PRIESTHOOD

IN

ANCIENT ISRAEL

COVENANT
Steven L. McKenzie

INCARNATION
Jon L. Berquist

PEACE
Walter Brueggemann

SABBATH AND JUBILEE
Richard H. Lowery

PRIESTHOOD IN ANCIENT ISRAEL
William R. Millar

PRIESTHOOD
IN
ANCIENT ISRAEL

WILLIAM R. MILLAR

All scripture quotations, unless otherwise indicated, are the author's translation. In Chronicles, Samuel, and Kings, these translations have been previously published in *Chronicles and Its Synmoptic Parellels in Samuel, Kings, and Related Biblical Texts,* ed. by John C. Endres, William R. Millar, and John Barclay Burns, Liturgical Press.

Biblical quotations marked *JPS* are taken from *The TANAKH, the new JPS translation according to the traditional Hebrew text,* copyright 1985 by the Jewish Publication Society. All Rights reserved. Used by permission.

Cover and interior design: Elizabeth Wright

This book is printed on acid-free, recycled paper.

Visit Chalice Press on the World Wide Web at
www.chalicepress.com

10 9 8 7 6 5 4 3 2 1   01 02 03

Library of Congress Cataloging–in–Publication Data

Millar, William R., 1938–
    Priesthood in ancient Israel / William R. Millar.
        p.   cm. — (Understanding biblical themes)
    Includes bibliographical references and index.
    ISBN 0-8272-3829-0 (alk. paper)
    1. Priests, Jewish.   2. Spirituality—Biblical teaching.   3. Bible.   O.T—
Criticism, interpretation, etc.   I. Title.   II. Series.
BS1199.P7 M55 2001
296.4'95 — dc21   2001002422

Printed in the United States of America

CONTENTS

PREFACE

One of the gifts of the postmodern era to us is the rediscovery of story as a mode of thinking. To be sure, the linear thinking that is associated with the modernist period and inspired by the Enlightenment does have the advantage of sustaining our focus on a particular line of argument to its conclusion. But story allows a speaker to access the multilayered nature of an experience, since it provides multiple points of entry. By shifting perspective, moving a reader to different spatial or temporal locations in a narrative world, the multidimensional reality of an event can be conveyed. Indeed, story can provide a terrain within which both author and reader meet and share in the creation of meaning. It becomes a medium of exchange.

In reading the introduction, the reader will note multiple statements of purpose: "One of the modest goals of this book is to add a few favorite passages to the list"; "Our primary agenda is to journey into those more underutilized regions in the Hebrew Bible"; "The goal of this work is to recover for Protestant Christians the spirituality of the priestly traditions of ancient Israel"; "This study proposes to show how and what the priestly traditions of ancient Israel can teach us about options they see open to us in the spiritual quest"; "The agenda of this book is to tap into the biblical narrative enough to illustrate the power of story to construct meaning within the complexities of life experience." Taken together these statements reflect the structure of an ongoing conversation.

Each of these statements represents an approach to the same topic from a slightly different stance. What one sees is relative to the stance of the question being asked. Multiple expressions of the question begin to reveal the layered dimensions of a subject's meaning. It is our claim that story operates this way as well.

When exploring the dimensions of meaning associated with the spiritual, in particular, story lends itself to the quest. When one reaches beyond the ordinary, the experiential reality of the sacred does not reduce itself easily to linear formulations. It is no accident that sacred texts such as the Bible are filled with story. Story has the capacity to liberate our seeing into an appreciation of the many-layered dimensions of meaning that spirit carries. Our interest in this study is to reconstruct the world of the priestly families generating these sacred stories in an effort to learn something of what they have to teach us about our own journeys.

How does one capture in writing the energy of a conversation that has engaged one's attention over the years? The chapter on apocalyptic goes back to my dissertation days and conversations about Isaiah 24—27 I engaged in with my thesis advisor Frank Moore Cross. He sparked my initial interest in trying to discover more about who these Levites were. It was Jon L. Berquist of Chalice Press who expressed interest and encouragement when our conversation turned to the Levites. He has been of great help in guiding me through the revision process and a constant source of encouragement along the way.

Colleagues and students at Linfield College in the religious studies department have provided many occasions to understand more fully what religion looks like in its institutional forms. Special thanks go to Stephen Snyder and Bill Apel for our ongoing conversations on Mushite Levites and Zadokite Aaronids in our Approaches to Religion course. These have been experiments in narrative building. Closely related have been the many spirited conversations with the Bereans at the First Baptist Church in McMinnville, Oregon. It is for such groups that I have written this book.

It was Raymond Peterson who drew me into the postmodern world and demonstrated how powerful narrative is as a tool to make sense out of things. He has helped me to see the world of the spirit in a new way. For his constant encouragement in this project I offer my thanks.

Over the years it has been the gift of support from my wife, Donna, that I treasure most. She has kept me human and reminded me often that there is a wholeness to life enriched by the capacity to laugh. She has read the manuscript many times, sometimes with more honesty than I wanted to hear. For her support, insight, and encouragement and that of the many others, I offer my thanks.

INTRODUCTION

Most of us have a copy of the Bible in our homes. And many of us would agree with the claim that the Bible is a reliable handbook for the spiritual life. In fact, that may be why we have a copy of our own. Yet many would agree that, except perhaps for a few favorite passages here and there, the Bible remains an extremely underutilized resource for our own spiritual journeys. One of the modest goals of this book is to add a few more favorite passages to the list.

Our primary agenda is to journey into those more underutilized regions in the Hebrew Bible; in this instance, to meet some of the priests of ancient Israel and to walk with them for a while along their spiritual pathways. We will discover that these priests of old have something to teach us about our spiritual lives. The surprise will be that the issues they dealt with sound strikingly similar to the life-issues we deal with today: What is the relationship between religion and politics? How does one discern the activity of God in daily happenings? Is it possible to construct a spiritual pathway that works for us in the wilderness experiences of life when we are faced with what feels like the absence of God? A big question voiced by Solomon in the book of Chronicles is, "Does God really dwell with man on

1

earth? Even the heavens to their uttermost reaches cannot contain you; how much less this house that I have built!" (2 Chron. 6:18).[1]

Still, you may ask, Why should we care about the spiritual traditions of priestly families within ancient Israel? Or another way to ask the question is, Why should we care about the priestly narratives of the Hebrew Bible, those sacred texts Christians call the Old Testament? Hasn't all that been replaced by the spirituality of Jesus and the New Testament? We will return to this question in the last chapter.

What has piqued my interest in biblical priests is the belief that the dominant culture of Protestant America does seem to understand and be aware of the prophets. We are a nation born of the Protestant Reformation, and our heroes are those who challenged the hierarchical authority of medieval church and empire. We still admire the rugged individualism of those who take the risks of challenging the status quo in response to a vision of a better and more egalitarian future. Most of us have at least heard the names of biblical prophets like Amos, Isaiah, Ezekiel, and Jeremiah, and we admire their independence.

We are not so sure about priests. Perhaps it is because the Sadducees and Pharisees of the New Testament are presented to us in a negative light. Perhaps it is the memory of oppression structured into the medieval church and empire that one day became a catalyst for our own nation's revolution. Priests, by definition, are religious figures committed to the structures of institutions. Some view institutionalized religion, in any faith, as a barrier to creativity and spontaneous experience, so we are not as familiar with the names of biblical priests like Abiathar, Zadok, Eli, and Hilkiah. Is it worth our time to learn their stories?

Yes it is, and a central reason is precisely because they have chosen to work within systems. They are committed to the structures of institutions such as church, temple, and synagogue, embedded as these are within the larger structures of state. Priests see themselves as keepers

---

[1]All translations of texts from Chronicles and 2 Samuel, 1 and 2 Kings, will be drawn from the synoptic parallels, which have also been translated synoptically, found in John C. Endres, William R. Millar, and John Barclay Burns, eds., *Chronicles and Its Synoptic Parallels in Samuel, Kings, and Related Biblical Texts* (Collegeville, Minn.: Liturgical Press, 1998). Unless indicated, all other translations will be the author's.

of the sacred stories and keepers of the sacred places. In that sense they are much like those of us who also struggle with the opportunities and frustrations offered by the communal life within our religious institutions. They allow us to address practical day-to-day issues such as, Is it possible to balance the needs we face for institutional maintenance—churches do cost money—with a sustained and inclusive vision that nurtures a spiritual pathway that is open to human need?

The goal of this work is to recover for Protestant Christians the spirituality of the priestly traditions of ancient Israel. As suggested above, Protestant Christians, perhaps Americans in general, readily identify with biblical prophets as figures who often stand outside the system, bearing witness to an independence and courage admired by those concerned about social justice and peace issues. To be sure, we need those called by God to a prophetic stance. Priests, however, are usually not so identified. They are often seen as part of the system, caught up in purity codes, rules, and laws—all of which appear to constrict, even oppress, the spirit. This study proposes to show how and what the priestly traditions of ancient Israel can teach us about options they see open to us in the spiritual quest.

We have modeled for us in the Old Testament at least two major styles of priestly spirituality, each with its own collection of sacred stories and linked to the narrative tradition of a priestly family. Each family believed it was called by God to lead. It is, I believe, as we seek to explore the inner dynamic of their respective narrative traditions that our own faith-sense of place and direction can be enriched.

Voice

We will soon discover that central to our search is going to be the matter of voice. We will see that voice is more than sound coming out of our mouths. Voice is that deep, inner sense of having a position on a topic, however controversial, of having something to say and being prepared to defend it in a public arena. We witnessed Mahatma Gandhi's use of his voice, nurtured in the culture of his native India and linked to political power, to become a catalyst for a nation to be reborn, throwing off the colonial status that had been imposed on the region for so many years. We witnessed Martin Luther King, Jr.'s application of many of the same nonviolent political strategies in the culture of the United States. It was when he gave voice to his vision for a united America that an energy swept the nation, challenging the structural violence of racism in our land. Mary Belenky and her colleagues in their book *Women's Ways of Knowing* describe in case history after case history the life-changing power that results when a woman discovers she can move out of a stance of silence; that she has a voice and can claim the right to be heard.[2]

We will see that voice is a concept whose richness requires related vocabulary to describe it. Notice in Robert Polzin's observations on voice and speech, within the context of his interpretation of First Samuel, how he speaks of utterance, story, words, point of view, ideology, meaning—and, one could add, discourse.

> The utterance of each voice speaking in the story provides a focal point for the intersecting words of others. The point of view represented by a single utterance of a single voice resonates with the words of others either in agreement or in opposition, with either emotive similarity or contrast. Loudly or faintly, we can perceive a cross-section of voices even when only a single person speaks in the text.[3]

> The voices…do not simply express individual ideologies in relation to one another; they represent social points of view that intersect each other in a variety of ways, forming what I call the implied author's story, the meaning (or meanings) of which is certainly a major task of the reader to discover or, as some would say, to invent.[4]

Similarly, we will learn from priests in ancient Israel that spirituality, at one level, is also a matter of voice. Spirituality embraces a process; indeed, the process is a journey that marks a pathway toward voice. It is a concentration of energy that charts a path through a narrative world. Voice assumes we have a sufficiently coherent vision

---

[2]Mary Belenky, Blythe Clinchy, Nancy Goldberger, and Jill Tarule, *Women's Ways of Knowing* (New York: Basic Books, 1986). They returned to the issue ten years later in a collection of essays revisiting some of the proposals offered in their 1986 book in Nancy Goldberger, Jill Tarule, Blythe Clinchy, and Mary Belenky, *Knowledge, Difference, and Power* (New York: Basic Books, 1996). For an excellent discussion of the connection between the preached word and voice, see Mary Donovan Turner and Mary Lin Hudson, *Saved from Silence: Finding Women's Voice in Preaching* (St. Louis: Chalice Press, 1999).

[3]Robert Polzin, *Samuel and the Deuteronomist. A Literary Study of the Deuteronomic History: Part 2, 1 Samuel* (San Francisco: Harper & Row, 1989), 19.

[4]Ibid., 21.

of a terrain that we can speak about it, and within it, meaningfully. Voice movement can be passive, simply receiving the description of a surface plane of perception conveyed by the narrator.

At other times, voice movement can be more active. Its energy level can pick up and gather sufficient momentum to travel through time and space as one gives voice to insight. As such, it can become quite sophisticated in its capacity to create, or deepen, narrative. Of particular interest to us as we listen to biblical storytellers is the phenomenon of reported speech.[5] Reported speech enables such travel through narrative space and time. Reported speech is speech within speech. In this instance, voice moves from one location to another to link with another speaker perhaps or to view an event from another geographical stance or time frame within the narrative. By reporting such speech, a voice path is created, along which energy is shared. That energy can bring new insight. Within a narrative world, layer upon layer of meaning deepens understanding for the interpretive community whose stories these are. To speak synchronically, that is, in an integrated and connected way—linked to an experiential center—is a source of healing. To silence voice is an oppressive act.

A Literary-Critical Approach

Central to religious tradition as it has developed in Western culture is the epic narrative of ancient Israel. Their story is recorded for us in what we now call the Hebrew Bible or Old Testament. From its roots have sprung three major faiths: Judaism, Christianity, and Islam. As with any of the world religions, over time the narrative discourse that crystallized in and is carried by its tradition becomes very complex and multifaceted. To keep in touch with a conscious awareness of how story can construct a narrative world within which to explore faith claims and the structures of personal and cultural identity one needs a reading strategy. Literary criticism has as its goal the constant reevaluation of strategy that can open up a text to its meaning—or perhaps better, its meanings—that reveals pattern upon pattern like petals of a flower.

The agenda of this book is to tap into the biblical narrative enough to illustrate the power of story at constructing meaning within the

---

[5]The phenomenon is described and discussed in V. N. Volosinov, *Marxism and the Philosophy of Language*, trans. Ladislav Metejka and I. R. Titunik (Cambridge, Mass.: Harvard University Press, 1986), 115–23.

complexities of life experience. To get at the modes of spirituality embodied by the various priestly families of ancient Israel—they being keepers of the sacred stories—we have chosen to compare the epic narrative of ancient Israel as told by the Chronicler in the books of 1 and 2 Chronicles with the telling of the same story as told by the so-called Deuteronomist responsible for 1 and 2 Kings.[6]

This particular study of the priesthood of ancient Israel will draw on a literary-critical theory that proposes a text can be multivoiced; that is, a narrative text can carry different meanings depending on the perspective used to approach the text.[7] We are concerned also to make every effort to understand a text first in its final, received form, before proposing multiple sources or documents as an explanation for apparent inconsistencies in a text.[8] We will take seriously story as a mode of thinking and illustrate how story can offer multiple forms of perception on an event or idea.[9] As indicated above, of particular interest to us will be an examination of the relationship between "reporting" and "reported" speech. Reporting speech is the narrator's voice appearing simply as the surface text. Reported speech is speech within speech and provides the narrator a literary device to create a meaning context for language. With reported speech one can penetrate surface planes of perception to earlier time periods and give expression to perceptions centered in different temporal or spatial planes, thereby opening up new points of entry into a narrative world. As we work through the text we will be offering suggestions as to who the respective "implied authors" may be or at least what social groups within the

[6]For a synoptic parallel that has also been translated synoptically, see John C. Endres, William R. Millar, and John Barclay Burns, eds., *Chronicles and Its Synoptic Parallels in Samuel, Kings, and Related Biblical Texts* (Collegeville, Minn.: Liturgical Press, 1998).

[7]We have found useful some of the suggestions for reading a text proposed by the Russian literary critic Mikhail Bakhtin and members of his school. See, for instance, his discussion of "dialogic imagination" in his *Problems of Dostoevsky's Poetics,* trans. and ed. Caryl Emerson (Minneapolis: University of Minnesota Press, 1984).

[8]Especially helpful in this regard is the work on the Deuteronomist by Polzin in what are now three volumes: *Moses and the Deuteronomist* (San Francisco: Harper & Row, 1980); *Samuel and the Deuteronomist* (San Francisco: Harper & Row, 1989); and *David and the Deuteronomist* (Bloomington, Ind.: Indiana University Press, 1993). See particularly the Samuel volume for a discussion of his use of the literary-critical theory of Bakhtin as an aid to interpretation over against other options offered by the more traditional historical-critical approaches to understanding a text.

[9]Boris Uspensky spells out different planes of perception in his analysis of what he calls a "poetics of composition." His insights are also useful for the biblical interpreter. See Uspensky, *A Poetics of Composition,* trans. Valentina Zavarin and Susan Wittig (Berkeley and Los Angeles, Calif.: University of California Press, 1973).

cultural life of ancient Israel would benefit from telling the story as it appears.[10]

As stated above, priestly families saw themselves as keepers of the sacred stories, as they understood them, and keepers of the sacred places insofar as they had the power to do so. Because institutions are a part of a larger social network, religious practice—then and now—extended into the political dynamics of the larger social order. For instance, as we meet some of the biblical priests, we will bring with us—and recognize in the text—many of the interconnections that form the network of our own cultural context. We will recognize such things as economic and political implications of religious positions.

There is an important assumption to our narrative approach to the Bible. We are assuming that the Bible, by means of its narrative, is a medium of exchange. We are being called into a conversation, invited to bring our voices into that conversation, within the narrative interchange afforded by story. Both our story and the Bible's story are enriched by the process. Meanings are created in the relationships established. Bridges of exchange are forged across the years as we connect with storytellers of old. Our faith is that the same God who inspired them inspires us as we share an interpretive community across the centuries. The truth we encounter at its most powerful is relational and experiential. It draws us into connection.

Normally priests served a maintenance function grounded in holy places. But if access to sanctuaries was cut off, for whatever reason, some priestly families viewed God's action in society from a peripheral stance, advocating transformation. Our thesis is that blocks of literary tradition reflect the social-political experience of the various priestly families. The formation and combination of the literary strata also reflect the politics of the priestly families.

To anticipate some of our conclusions: We will see in the priests' telling of their stories two ways of pursuing what we are calling a spiritual pathway. We will show how the narrative in Chronicles appears to be shaped by a hierarchical quest for purity, whereas the

---

[10]An implied author is a term referring to the circumstance where the reader doesn't really know who the author is. This is often the case in biblical texts. Interpreters make proposals based on internal evidence in the text, hence "implied." The implied author and narrator within a text may or may not be the same person. The same problem emerges when trying to determine an audience. The implied audience would be the audience of the implied author. That audience may or may not be the same as the named audience in the text. The reader refers to us as reader of the text.

narrative in Kings seems to find shape for its discourse in the world of relationships. We will see the differences connected to the respective social experience of two priestly families in ancient Israel as they tell their stories. In particular, we will argue that their experience with political power has shaped their perceptions.

1

MEETING ABIATHAR AND ZADOK

To start our exploration, two priests from 1 Kings 1—2 provide a good introduction: Abiathar and Zadok. Using the metaphor of the Bible as a medium of exchange, if we can think of the Bible as a magnetic field of electronic energy composed of network upon network of connections, we can begin to sense the scope of story's narrative space. It is a space wherein voice and word can come alive. We, of course, bring our voices to the setting; but the story also contains the energy of the narrator, frozen on the printed page as it were, waiting to be activated in all of its life-giving power. Each of the characters in the narrative world, within their own time and space, wait to be resurrected by the medium of word to participate in the creation of meaning.

The priests Abiathar and Zadok are two such characters in this narrative world. As we are invited into the story to meet them, part of us is activated in the interaction. The story is incomplete without our participation. We build relationships with the characters. Some we like, others we don't. Contrary to earlier assumptions about Bible study, we are not neutral observers who can stand outside a text. As we read and begin to engage the story, we become part of it. As in a crowded room, the text can become multivoiced. Many points of view can be contained in a story. The question we face is whether or not we can discern the voice of the implied author who controls the telling of the story, the one controlling the voice of the narrator.

As a working hypothesis in our point of entry into the world of priests, we will assume that the dominant story in Kings is being told from the perspective of Abiathar of the family of Mushite Levite priests. As in any set of relationships, it will take awhile to feel what that means, much as it requires some life experience in the United States to feel the impact of the Kennedys or the Rockefellers on American culture. Mushite is an adjective built from the name of Moses. Levite identifies someone from the tribe of Levi. So a Mushite Levite is someone from the tribe of Levi who traced his or her family genealogy back to Moses as the founding ancestor of the family. We will learn that, at some point in ancient Israelite history, to be a priest required a genealogical connection to the tribe of Levi.

We will notice that the narrator can move us as reader around the narrative world, both temporally and spatially, by means of speech—and speech within speech. We can find ourselves in a private space; other times we are in a public space with respect to the other characters. It is our claim that these details of narrative time and space constructed by the narrator's speech are clues to the meanings being constructed. Part of the construct is our perception added to the mix. Others reading or hearing the same story may construct different meanings. The richness of story is that many meanings can be correct and faithful to the text. The text can be multivoiced.

To understand the priesthood and the spirituality of priests, we must enter into the network of relationships created by the narrative world of the storyteller. We will see that the priests' relationship to and perception of their king is part of their sense of who they were. It will often be the case that a narrative, in either Samuel/Kings or Chronicles—even though the content is focused on a king—will reflect an assessment of that king that embodies the values and spirituality of the priestly family and implied author telling the story. Fundamental to our approach is the claim that the stories about kings in Samuel/ Kings and Chronicles often tell us more about priests than they tell us about kings. At the very least, we are seeing the king through the lens of the storyteller.

Abiathar and Zadok were brought into office by King David. As suggested above, in the book of Kings, we hear the story told from the perspective of one of the priests, namely Abiathar. The temporal context of the narrative is the period of Solomon's rise to power. Even in this telling of the story, it will become clear that the respective spiritual pathways of Abiathar and Zadok were shaped by their experience of political power centered in the kings of the monarchy.

Kings of Judah and Israel [1]

UNITED MONARCHY		
Saul		
David (1000–961 B.C.E.)	Abiathar and Zadok	High priests
Solomon (961–922)	First Temple	Zadok as high priest
		Abiathar banished
	Civil War	
Judah (South)	DIVIDED MONARCHY	**Israel (North)**
Rehoboam	Shishak (Egypt)	Jeroboam I

Abiathar

The narrator opens the first book of Kings by taking the reader to a private space, namely King David's bedroom. In so doing, we are witnesses to a perspective on David—and thus on kingship—not normally witnessed by the general public. We see David grown old and frail. He cannot keep warm. We witness advice offered to him by servants, not official officers of the state. "Let them search for a girl, a virgin, for my lord the king...let her lie in your bosom and my lord the king will keep warm" (1 Kgs. 1:2). So they find Abishag the Shunammite and bring her to the king to serve him "but the king did not know her sexually" (1 Kgs. 1:2). Some have argued the meaning of the latter is to be read "could not know her sexually," thereby

---

[1]Moses and his older brother Aaron were from the tribe of Levi. They are figures from the wilderness period and therefore two hundred years prior to Abiathar and Zadok. Abiathar would be a Levite who traced his lineage back to Moses; Zadok was a Levite who traced his lineage back to Aaron. Also relevant to the discussion that follows is that David's first four sons, in order of birth, were Amnon, Absalom, Adonijah, and Solomon. At this point in the narrative, Adonijah is the eldest living son of David.

signaling it is time to find a new king.[2] David no longer embodied the virility required to fill the office of kingship. Immediately thereafter we read of Adonijah, one of David's sons, taking steps in a public space to assume the throne saying, "I will be king" (1 Kgs. 1:5).

The book of Kings opens, therefore, on an insecure note. If we understand that, in addition to administering economic and military control of a kingdom, one of the roles of a king is to establish a political discourse within which even religious language derives its meaning, shifts in that larger context threaten stability at many levels. We are moving into that period between kings when the successor to David has not yet been fully determined. Or if it has, Adonijah has not been made fully aware of it. The power of kingship itself was vulnerable, rising close to the surface of public discourse. By allowing us to enter into the private space of the king, the narrator is also letting us witness that Israel's heroes—like David—are not invincible, not perfect. They can grow old and frail. They can become subject to political maneuvering by those in power surrounding the king. This maneuvering operates in the arena of political discourse and voice. Among other things, a pretender to the throne must gain control of the public discourse. His or her voice must take charge of the public perception of king and kingdom.

The scene shifts to Adonijah. His assumption that he would succeed David as king is not without some merit. He was the eldest living son of David, having been born next after Absalom, and apparently he had never been told by David that he would not succeed him. The narrator does tell us, "He was a very handsome man," (1 Kgs. 1:6). That, however, reminds us of comparable statements having been made about Saul and Absalom, both opponents of David, neither of whom worked out as king. The narrator reports a speech given by God to Samuel, who was looking for a successor to Saul in Jesse's son Eliab. YHWH said, "Do not look on his [Eliab's] appearance or on the height of his stature, because I have rejected him; for the LORD does not see as mortals see; they look on the outward appearance, but the LORD looks on the heart" (1 Sam. 16:7).

Still, Adonijah did take steps to build a power base to support his bid for kingship. Supporters included Joab, son of Zeruiah, from the military and Abiathar from the priesthood. "But the priest Zadok,

---

[2] See, for instance, Richard Elliott Friedman, *The Hidden Book in the Bible* (San Francisco: Harper San Francisco, 1998), 295.

and Benaiah son of Jehoiada [from the military], and the prophet Nathan…and David's own warriors did not side with Adonijah" (1 Kgs. 1:8). Thus, the narrator has brought the reader to the stance of witnessing a political power struggle between supporters of Adonijah and supporters of Solomon with at least a hint that Adonijah is going to lose, particularly if all he has going for him is the fact that he is handsome.

We return to the scene of the king's bedroom to witness the elaborate scheme orchestrated by Nathan and Bathsheba to convince David to name Solomon as his successor before he dies. The complexity of the plot is reflected in the intricate use of reported speech within speech. The narrator quotes Nathan to Bathsheba: "Have you not heard that Adonijah…has become king and our lord David doesn't know it?…Let me give you advice, so that you may save your own life and the life of your son Solomon" (1 Kgs. 1:11–12). Nathan then created a speech Bathsheba was to give to David within which is reported an earlier speech David had given to Bathsheba promising her that Solomon would succeed him as king. Bathsheba is to say to David, "Did you not, my lord the king, swear to your servant, saying, 'Your son Solomon shall succeed me as king, and he shall sit on my throne'? Why then is Adonijah king?" (1 Kgs. 1:13).

Then Nathan told Bathsheba he would enter the king's bedroom to confirm her words, and so it happened. Bathsheba added these words to David, "The eyes of all Israel are on you to tell them who should sit on the throne of my lord the king after him" (1 Kgs. 1:20). David responded, "Your son Solomon shall succeed me as king, and he shall sit on my throne in my place" (1 Kgs. 1:30).

David then gave instructions for the anointing of Solomon as his successor to include a parade through Jerusalem on the king's mule and an anointing at the spring called Gihon. Left out in the ceremony, of course, were supporters of Adonijah, including Joab, son of Zeruiah, and Abiathar the priest. Abiathar had supported the wrong candidate.

Jonathan, Son of Abiathar

Meanwhile, elsewhere in Jerusalem by the stone Zoheleth, which is beside En-rogel, Adonijah had sacrificed sheep, oxen, and fatted cattle. He was making an effort to maneuver himself into position so that he would be the one to take control of the political discourse on kingship. He had invited all his brothers, the king's sons, and all the royal officials of Judah. Note that the spatial location of the narrative is Jerusalem. The tension between the two groups of supporters is heightened by the fact that they are within earshot of each other. The noise of one can catch the attention of the other.

When the supporters of Adonijah had finished feasting, with their noise subsiding, Joab heard the great noise coming from that part of Jerusalem celebrating Solomon's inauguration as king. He asked, "Why is the city in an uproar?" (1 Kgs. 1:41). At this point Jonathan, son of Abiathar, entered with a message.

This scene of a messenger coming with news for a royal figure recalls the Amalekite bringing the message of Saul's death to David and the two messengers from Israel, Baanah and Rechab, bringing news to David of the death of Ish-bosheth, Saul's son and successor over northern Israel. David's response to the two men from Israel was, "As YHWH lives who has redeemed my life from every adversity, when the one who informed me, saying, 'See, Saul is dead,' and he had thought himself a bearer of good news, I seized him and I killed him at Ziklag, that I might give him a reward [for such good news]! How much more, when wicked men have killed a righteous man in his house on his bed. Should I not now require his blood from your hand and exterminate you from the earth!" (2 Sam. 4:9–11). We note here how the king is in a position to shape the direction of discourse by deciding—quite literally—who does and who does not have voice.

The narrator constructs the scene involving Adonijah and Jonathan in such a way that one can see a number of reversals, particularly with the other messenger–royal scenes in mind. First is the context of noise and silence. As the feast celebrating Adonijah's inauguration winds down and is finished, the noise from the other celebration is heard by participants in Adonijah's festivities. Adonijah is the royal figure, the recipient of a message. He thinks he is about to become king; but it will not be so. He tells Bathsheba later: "You know that the kingdom was mine, and that all Israel expected me to reign; however, the kingdom has turned about and become my brother's" (1 Kgs. 2:15). He would learn from Jonathan, son of Abiathar, that it was Solomon who had become king. Appearance and reality in the earlier tension between Saul and David over kingship—and thus who will establish the political discourse of the kingdom—reappears here between Adonijah and Solomon. Even after David received what he publicly called the bad news of Saul's death, one cannot help but wonder if privately David received the message as good news. Saul had pursued David as an outlaw, and now he was removed as an obstacle toward David's assumption of kingship. Similarly, David's public grief over the death of Ish-bosheth seems to be double-voiced.

Now Adonijah, celebrating his rise to kingship, discovers he is not king. It is instructive that Jonathan, a son of Abiathar, should be the messenger. On the surface one would expect good news from a priestly supporter. Adonijah said, "Come in, for you are a worthy man and surely you bring good news" (1 Kgs. 1:42). Jonathan reveals, however, that it is bad news for Adonijah. We shall see that it is also bad news for Abiathar, since Solomon will dismiss Abiathar from his role as priest. The noise and silence of the scene take on added significance for the supporters of Adonijah. Abiathar and those linked to his priestly family will also be silenced.

Jonathan reported a speech by David within the context of his message that carries a double voice for the reader. David said, "Blessed be the LORD, the God of Israel, who today has granted one of my off-spring to sit on my throne and permitted me to witness it" (1 Kgs. 1:48). This is obviously good news for the supporters of Solomon. Solomon has received the blessing of both YHWH and David.

But the narrator, by allowing the reader into the private space of David's bedroom and the memory of David's earlier public statements in response to messengers, opens the door to at least the possibility of a concealed message in the narrative. David was old and frail and vulnerable to the political manipulation of those in power around him. Nathan and Bathsheba were successful in manipulating David's will in their favor. The text tells us that David had given Adonijah no indication that he would not succeed him as eldest son. Adonijah had been caught by surprise.

Abiathar would be silenced by the noise of Solomon's party and Solomon's heavy-handed dismissal of Abiathar as priest, but that—in Abiathar's, and possibly the narrator's, view—would not be YHWH's will. In another part of Jerusalem, as it were, the Mushite Levites, as supporters of Adonijah, would find a way to voice God's will, even though for now "all the guests of Adonijah got up trembling and went their own ways" (1 Kgs. 1:49).

Just before David died he called in Solomon and offered advice to his successor. This would be another instance of a speech not intended for a public audience, but rather an occasion for the narrator to bring the reader into a space behind closed doors. It provides the reader with a stance to perceive a concealed speech within the narrative; we can see an instance of the multiple voices operative in the narrative. From David's side the speech deals with some unfinished business. From Solomon's side, just as David before him, we learn that Solomon would find it necessary to deal with his opponents.

Joab was one of those who sided with Adonijah, so Joab is a powerful figure who will have to be dealt with. In spite of the many instances in which Joab was David's protector during his reign, David offers a public rationale to Solomon for getting rid of him. Joab had killed Abner and Amasa, both potential problems for David; but Joab is presented as one who did so for personal reasons, "retaliating in time of peace for blood that had been shed in war" (1 Kgs. 2:5). Joab avenged the death of his brother Asahel, who had been killed by Abner. Later, when Joab received word of Solomon's intent, he sought sanctuary by grasping the horns of the altar in YHWH's tent. Solomon instructed Benaiah, son of Jehoiada, "Strike him down and bury him; and thus take away from me and from my father's house the guilt for the blood that Joab shed without cause...he attacked and killed with the sword two men more righteous and better than himself, Abner son of Ner, commander of the army of Israel, and Amasa son of Jether, commander of the army of Judah" (1 Kgs. 2:31–32).

Similarly, Shemei had cursed David in his retreat from Jerusalem in the days of Absalom's revolt. "Therefore do not hold him guiltless, for you are a wise man; you will know what you ought to do to him, and you must bring his gray head down with blood to Sheol" (1 Kgs. 2:9). The sentence for Shemei was that he should never leave Jerusalem. After three years, however, he did leave the city to retrieve two of his slaves. Solomon arrested him and said, "You know in your own heart all the evil that you did to my father David; so YHWH will bring back your evil on your own head. But King Solomon shall be blessed, and the throne of David shall be established before YHWH forever. Then the king commanded Benaiah son of Jehoiada; and he went out and struck him down, and he died" (1 Kgs. 2:44–46).

Interestingly, David did not provide a rationale for Solomon to dismiss Abiathar, though it was clear from Solomon's perspective that he was not one who could be kept close to the center of power. Solomon would have to look elsewhere for a public rationale to deal with Abiathar.

Abiathar and Eli

There is a speech from a man of God to Eli in 1 Samuel 2:27–36. It offers us some data as to the identity of the priestly house of Eli. The man of God quotes YHWH, "Thus the Lord has said, 'I revealed myself to the family of your ancestor in Egypt when they were slaves to the house of Pharaoh. I chose him out of all the tribes of Israel to be my priest, to go up to my altar, to offer incense, to wear an ephod before me; and I gave to the family of your ancestor all my offerings by fire from the people of Israel'" (1 Sam. 2:27–28). In Deuteronomy 33:10, in the blessing by Moses of the various tribes of Israel, we read of Levi: "They teach Jacob your ordinances, and Israel your law; they place incense before you, and whole burnt offerings on your altar." The mention of Pharaoh's house and the choice of Eli's ancestor as a priest from the tribe of Levi selected to ascend the altar would suggest that the person referred to by the man of God was Moses. When David conferred with Solomon just before his death, he said, "Be strong, be courageous, and keep the charge of YHWH your God, walking in his ways and keeping his statutes, his commandments, his ordinances, and his testimonies, as it is written in the law of Moses, so that you may prosper in all that you do and wherever you turn" (1 Kgs. 2:3). If the priest referred to by the man of God in his speech to Eli is Moses, then Eli stands in the Mushite Levite tradition, Mushite being a reference to priests of the tribe of Levi who traced their lineage back to Moses. As presented at this point in the narrative, Mushite Levites would be a family with full priestly credentials. The location of Eli at Shiloh and the carrying of the ark would also connect Eli's family with Mushite Levites.

But there is a problem with Eli's sons and their worthiness to carry on the tradition after Eli. Hophni and Phinehas take food for themselves that was intended for YHWH; and they lie with women working at the entrance of the tent of meeting. The man of God continues, "Why then look with greedy eye at my sacrifices and my offerings that I commanded, and honor your sons more than me by fattening yourselves on the choicest parts of every offering of my people Israel?" (1 Sam. 2:29). The narrative affirms that God decided to withdraw his support from Eli's priestly house because of the actions of his sons Hophni and Phinehas. Not only will they die, but "I will raise up for myself a faithful priest, who shall do according to what is in my heart and in my mind. I will build him a sure house, and he shall go in and out before my anointed one forever" (1 Sam. 2:35).

Robert Polzin has argued that the immediate context for the speech by the man of God was to prepare Eli for the downfall of his priestly house and the rise of Samuel as his priestly successor.[3] Samuel's connection to his father Elkanah would make Samuel an Ephraimite, not a Levite, and his leadership role would extend into the responsibilities associated with judge and prophet, as well. There is sufficient allusion, however, to sacred place and priestly function for this prophecy against Eli to be useful to Solomon. It is not unusual in tradition for prophetic statements such as that from the man of God to be reapplied in subsequent time periods for different purposes.

Solomon needed a public rationale for dismissing Abiathar. Abiathar, too, was associated with Shiloh; Solomon referred to Abiathar's carrying the ark of the covenant for David. Abiathar was among the priests of Nob who had fled to Nob after the destruction of Shiloh by the Philistines. Abiathar was the only priest at Nob who escaped the massacre ordered by Saul and was offered security by the outlaw David. All the indications would point to Abiathar as also belonging to the priestly family of Mushite Levites.

It would serve David's political agenda to have Abiathar as one of his supporters, since Abiathar carried the *ephod* and thus could inquire of God when needed. Also when David would move to extend his kingdom from Judah and Hebron to include the northern tribes, Abiathar would be recognized as one from the ancient and northern sanctuary of Shiloh with credentials among Mushite Levites. Northerners would be assured that the new monarchy being constructed by David would include their voice.

Solomon, however, would view Abiathar differently because Abiathar had supported Adonijah in the succession of kingship. Like Joab, he could no longer be trusted. It would not do to kill Abiathar, as he had Adonijah and Joab. Instead Solomon banished Abiathar to his estate in Anathoth. "The king said to the priest Abiathar, 'Go to Anathoth, to your estate; for you deserve death. But I will not at this time put you to death, because you carried the ark of YHWH God before my father David, and because you shared in all the hardships

---

[3]Robert Polzin, *Samuel and the Deuteronomist. A Literary Study of the Deuteronomic History: Part 2, 1 Samuel* (San Francisco: Harper & Row, 1989), 42–43.

my father endured.' So Solomon banished Abiathar from being priest
to YHWH, thus fulfilling the word of YHWH that he had spoken
concerning the house of Eli in Shiloh" (1 Kgs. 2:26–27). Solomon
had his public rationale. The Mushite Levite priestly house had been
silenced. "The king put the priest Zadok in the place of Abiathar"
(1 Kgs. 2:35).

Again, because the reader has had the benefit of witnessing, in
nonpublic spaces, the political maneuvering of David and Solomon
and those around them, the implied author and/or narrator could be
concealing a message to the reader that is contrary to the surface
message. To be sure, it was Solomon's will that Abiathar be dismissed.
But it is not as clear that it was also YHWH's will. The Mushite Levites
had been marginalized by Solomon's action. The economic
implications for Mushite Levites are reflected in the man of God's
speech to Eli referred to earlier: "Everyone who is left in your family
[that is, Eli's] shall come to implore him [the reliable priest] for a
piece of silver or a loaf of bread, and shall say, 'Please put me in one of
the priest's places, that I may eat a morsel of bread'" (1 Sam. 2:36).
The primary means of economic support for a priest and his family
was through offerings brought to a sanctuary. To be prohibited access
to a sanctuary cut off his and his family's food supply and immediately
placed them in a dependency status.

Rehoboam and Jeroboam

The narrator continues to describe how the priestly family of
Mushite Levites was cut off from access to the holy places, not only
once by Solomon in his dismissal of Abiathar, but again by Jeroboam.
Robert Polzin makes an excellent observation during his discussion
of the fall of Eli's house, "I am suggesting, therefore, that these early
stories about the fall of the House of Eli and the rise of Samuel, in
addition to having inherent interest in themselves, form a kind of
parabolic [that is, as a parable] introduction to the Deuteronomic
history of kingship. Both Eli's house and its successor, Samuel's house,
like the rich man in Nathan's parable, are stand-ins for royalty."[4]

As Eli fell off his stool, overweight and blind, so do we see the
united kingdom beginning to fracture toward the end of Solomon's
reign. His many wives turned his heart after other gods to the point

---

[4]Ibid., 44.

that "Solomon was building a high place for Chemosh, the filth of Moab, on the mountain which is east of Jerusalem, and for Molech, the filth of the Ammonites" (1 Kgs. 11:7).

YHWH then said to Solomon, "Since it has been this way with you, and you did not keep my covenant and my statutes which I commanded you I will surely tear the kingdom from you and I will give it to your servant" (1 Kgs. 11:11). One of Solomon's officials, Jeroboam, "a mighty man of valor...overseer over all the forced labor of the house of Joseph" (1 Kgs. 11:28), raised his hand against the king. Since the house of Joseph is a reference to the northern tribes of Ephraim and Manasseh, it is not surprising that a certain prophet from the north, Ahijah of Shiloh, should appear voicing the displeasure of YHWH against the policies of Solomon. That Israelites should be subject to forced labor—not by Pharaoh of Egypt as of old, but by one of their own—was intolerable. The kingdom was beginning to fall apart, at this point on the brink of civil war. "Ahijah grasped the new garment which was on him [Jeroboam], and tore it into twelve...pieces. Then he said to Jeroboam, 'Take for yourself ten torn pieces,' for thus says YHWH the God of Israel, 'Behold, I am tearing the kingdom from the hand of Solomon, and I will give you ten tribes'" (1 Kgs. 11:30–31).

This narrative reversal of fortune makes sense when viewed from the stance of an interpretive community centered in Shiloh. Eli was located in Shiloh. In order to formulate a public rationale for the dismissal of Abiathar, Solomon linked the prophecy against the house of Eli with Abiathar, a priest also connected with Shiloh. Now, in the presence of intolerable political and economic circumstances, Ahijah of Shiloh announced YHWH's decision to bring down Solomon's house. We see that Eli's worthless sons are paralleled in the ineptness of Solomon's son Rehoboam.

Elders from Israel approached Rehoboam and said, "Your father made our yoke hard, but you now, lighten the hard servitude of your father and his heavy yoke that he has put upon us, then we will serve you" (1 Kgs. 12:4). A council of elders in Judah did advise Rehoboam to lighten up. Instead, Rehoboam chose to follow the advice of younger men with whom he had grown up in the palace, "My father loaded upon you a heavy yoke...I will add to your yoke; my father controlled you with whips, but I will control you with scorpions" (1 Kgs. 12:11). And so Israel responded, under the leadership of Jeroboam, "To your

tents, O Israel! What portion is there for us in David?" (1 Kgs. 12:15).
All this to fulfill YHWH's word spoken through Ahijah of Shiloh.

Mushite Levite priests, however, would find that their anticipation
of being restored to active employment at reopened sanctuaries of the
north would not come to be. Jeroboam turned out to be just as
insensitive to their position as had Solomon. Jeroboam "made priests
from among the people who were not from the Levites" (1 Kgs. 12:31).
One of the reopened sanctuaries, at Bethel, was cursed by a man of
God from Judah. "Even after this incident Jeroboam did not turn
from his evil way, but he went on and made priests for the high places
from among the people; anyone who desired, he ordained as priests
for the high places" (1 Kgs. 13:33). This practice became sin to the
house of Jeroboam (1 Kgs. 13:34).

In terms of a spiritual pathway, the priestly family of Mushite
Levites was once again forced into a wilderness experience; like
Abiathar, they were being silenced by those who held political power.
Their challenge would be, Could they experience and give voice to
the hand of God in the turn of events they had to face? Is there a
discernible spiritual pathway that is at home in the wilderness? Since
there are times when we, too, experience what feels like the absence
of God, it is worth the effort on our part to hear what Abiathar and
the Mushite Levites have to say about the spiritual life.

When compared with Chronicles, the narrative in Kings reflects
a different social space. It is with the figure of Abiathar and the Mushite
Levites that we have a window to a voice from the margin of ancient
Israelite life. To be sure, that voice needs to be reconstructed. Still,
Abiathar and the Mushite Levites from a peripheralized social space
would have had reason to humanize the narrative, name the powers,
and redefine the holy in terms of healing—all of which are
characteristics of the Deuteronomistic narrative. It is true that the
narrative has been written over by the dominant voice coming from
Jerusalem in Solomon's day, but the authority of Moses and David in
tradition have assured that it was not silenced completely.

Zadok

"And the king [Solomon] put the priest Zadok in the place of
Abiathar" (1 Kgs. 2:35). Such a simple statement, and yet the social
ramifications were enormous. From Zadok's point of view it was like
receiving an acceptance letter for admission into a very selective college,

or landing the highly desirable and well-paying job in one's field, or getting the government contract that enables one to continue research on a project with all the resources needed available. For Zadok the door was opened to run affairs at the temple with the king's blessing. Whereas Abiathar had been dismissed, Zadok was given the go-ahead, the green light.

This meant for Zadok and those associated with him in the priestly profession that they would develop a spirituality quite different from that of the Mushite Levites. The Zadokites operated within the system. They could define the boundaries for what counted as the sacred, and they had the power to maintain the system. Issues of class and power would influence the Zadokite formulation of their spiritual pathway.

To be sure, for those outside the system, this linkage of the trappings of religion with political power is often experienced negatively. Much of the negative Protestant Christian attitude toward the priestly traditions referred to earlier no doubt stems from those at the lower end of, or outside, the priestly hierarchical ladder. Before we go into a critique of this form of spirituality, we need to let it have its say. What kind of discourse did the Zadokites create in their attempt to give voice to YHWH's activity in their midst? What values would the Zadokite priestly family affirm and defend?

A text that offers us a point of entry into this mode of spirituality is the prayer of dedication recorded in 2 Chronicles 6:1—7:10 offered by Solomon on the occasion of the completion of the building of the temple. At the conclusion of the prayer the narrator described a theophany—that is, an experiential manifestation—of YHWH envisioned as fire. For the Mushite Levites, as voiced by the Deuteronomist, the theophany par excellence occurred within the expanse of the wilderness *outside* at Mount Horeb. The entire mountain was aflame as YHWH voiced his word to the people of Israel—who in YHWH's presence received the Ten Commandments—which became the heart of the Mosaic vision (Deut. 5).

For the Zadokites, however, a parallel theophany occurred *inside,* within the structured space of the temple. "When Solomon had ended his prayer, fire came down from heaven and consumed the burnt offering and the sacrifice; and the glory of YHWH filled the temple. The priests could not enter the house of YHWH, because the glory of YHWH filled YHWH's house. When all the people of Israel saw the fire come down and the glory of YHWH on the temple, they bowed down on the pavement with their faces to the ground, and worshipped and gave thanks to YHWH saying, 'For he is good, for his steadfast love endures forever'" (2 Chron. 7:1–3).

When one is part of a team, as it were, the issue is no longer an issue of participation. The drive now is to produce. One is called to discipline and excellence. In the world of spirituality, as in any other endeavor, discipline requires focus nurtured in a controlled space. Unnecessary distractions need to be held at a distance. Since the arena of the spiritual quest encompasses the infinity of an inner universe, we who are still in our finite bodily forms must return to the task again and again. The patterned behavior of ritual allows us to disengage from the distractions of the mundane and secular to resume, once again, our focus and energy for the inner journey. Over time the sacred space created by such a community of seekers becomes very rarified; indeed, its silent structures become perceptible to an elite few. It is inevitable that this way of being religious will become un-"popular," that is, inaccessible to the many. However much it may be admired from afar, there will be identifiable layers or levels of participation permitted. Spirituality, too, has its range of "classified information" accessible only to those with the proper credentials, and the Zadokites were in a position to establish those credentials.

Solomon's Prayer

The narrator of Chronicles brings us into the public space of the temple, which is not an ordinary space. Appropriately, it is the king who offers the prayer of dedication, but even Solomon as a secular figure can only go so far into the inner reaches of this space. At the heart is YHWH himself. Solomon said, "YHWH has said that he would reside in thick darkness" (2 Chron. 6:1). To make YHWH accessible to Israel, Solomon built him a house: "I have built you [YHWH] an exalted house, a place for you to reside in forever" (1 Chron. 6:2).

In the Chronicler's narrative, the use of speech within speech has the effect of moving ever more deeply into the narrative content of the temple's holy space. The building's structures remain solid and like a foundation, while the believer moves through time and space toward YHWH, by means of speech. "Solomon turned around and blessed all the assembly of Israel, while all the assembly of Israel stood. And he said, 'Blessed be YHWH, the God of Israel, who with his hand has fulfilled what he promised with his mouth to my father David, saying…" (2 Chron. 6:3–4). Note that the narrator brings the reader into the temple. Then Solomon speaks, moving earlier in time, to a speech YHWH made to David. Within the context of that speech, YHWH makes reference to yet an earlier event, that of the exodus, located in Egypt before either Jerusalem or the temple had been chosen for his name to reside in. "To my father David, saying, 'Since the day that I brought my people out of the land of Egypt, I have not chosen a city from any of the tribes of Israel in which to build a house, so that my name might be there, and I chose no one as ruler over my people Israel; but [now] I have chosen Jerusalem in order that my name may be there, and I have chosen David to be over my people Israel'" (2 Chron. 6:5–6).

Then Solomon quotes God, saying that David was not to be the one to build YHWH's house, "'but your son who shall be born to you shall build the house for my name'" (2 Chron. 6:9). Then the voice of Solomon returns to the sanctity of the present: "Now YHWH has fulfilled his promise that he made; for I have succeeded my father David, and sit on the throne of Israel, as YHWH promised, and have built the house for the name of YHWH, the God of Israel" (2 Chron. 6:10). Within that setting the movable icon of the earlier period, the ark of the covenant, was to be placed within the present stationary setting of the temple: "There I have set the ark, in which is the covenant of YHWH that he made with the people of Israel" (2 Chron. 6:11).

The mystery is voiced by Solomon: "Does God really dwell with man on earth? Even the heavens to their uttermost reaches cannot contain you; how much less this house that I have built!" (2 Chron. 6:18). Yet this house is to be the visible point of contact between YHWH in his heavenly abode and his presence on earth. That makes this space holy indeed, and this priestly family in charge of God's house a highly select group. Can one construct a system of protocol that has as its goal an interchange with God, the author of the universe itself?

All the trappings of monarchic protocol are but a springboard toward an experiential approach to God. Interestingly, the Hebrew word for palace is the same word as for temple. In the royal mind-set God's house has all the structures of the king's palace and more. The king had his messenger system; there were procedures for petition and response when dealing with matters of state. It is but a short step to recognize that those same procedures would give structure to affairs in God's house. Solomon gave expression to this messenger system that leads from state to king to God: "May your eyes be open day and night toward this house, toward the place where you have resolved to make your name abide; may you heed the prayers that your servant offers toward this place. And when you hear the supplications that your servant and your people Israel offer toward this place, give heed in your heavenly abode—give heed and pardon" (2 Chron. 6:20–21).

Then Solomon offered as illustration suitable issues for prayer brought to God, and they bear a close resemblance to the daily issues a king would face. "If a man commits an offense against his fellow...take action to judge your servants" (2 Chron. 6:22–23). If Israel should lose land in battle against an enemy, but they approach God seeking forgiveness for their sin, "Restore them to the land you gave them and to their fathers" (2 Chron. 6:25). Since God controls the weather and there is drought, when the people seek forgiveness, "Send rain down upon the land that you gave to your people as their heritage" (2 Chron. 6:27). Issues of personal health, war, captivity, even aliens with requests, are all legitimate concerns to be brought to God's house. "Deal with each man according to his ways as you know his heart to be—for you alone know the hearts of all men—so that they may revere you all the days that they live on the land you gave to our fathers" (2 Chron. 6:30–31).

As in any house, there is also a protocol for meals. In the royal palace there would be a range of meals from the more informal to official dinners of state.[5] So too in God's house. The preparation of food for a dinner at which God is present requires special attention. Similarly, special precautions would need to be taken to assure the suitability of all the other guests present. Since God is absolutely pure and cannot by nature tolerate the presence of impurity, ritual procedures were created to assure that at God's table everything and everyone was honorably presented, certainly suitable for a king, but in this instance more.

The narrator indicates that YHWH was pleased after Solomon's audience with the divine king: "YHWH appeared to Solomon at night and said to him, 'I have heard your prayer and have chosen this site as

---

[5]For an excellent discussion of reading the sacrificial system centered at the temple as a protocol for meals in the presence of God, see Baruch A. Levine, *Leviticus*, The JPS Torah Commentary (Philadelphia: Jewish Publication Society, 1989), 3–47.

my house of sacrifice'" (2 Chron. 7:12). It would remain to the Zadokites the charge to run this house with all the discipline, efficiency, and decorum that one would expect to be suitable for a god.

Zadok and Aaron

The primary organizational unit for society operative in ancient Israel was the household. This was the primary economic, political, and social unit of the country. Family and family honor were the primary mediums of exchange.[6] So to be in charge of God's house would require that those who worked there would have impeccable family credentials. One's genealogy functioned for citizens of ancient Israel much as one's employment resumé functions in our culture.

When the Zadokites came to power under Solomon, this raised the question for some about their credentials to serve in that high office so close to the presence of God. Certainly Mushite Levites would wonder about Zadokite suitability for the position. So some within the Zadokite priestly circles had to sort out the issue of credentials. It was clear that Solomon felt that Zadok should be in charge; but was it also YHWH's will?

Abiathar's legitimacy during David's day was established by Abiathar's genealogical connection to Moses from the wilderness period, and it was widely recognized that all priests must be from the tribe of Levi. Did Zadok meet these criteria?

The genealogy of Zadok has been the topic of debate even among contemporary scholars. There is very little information to resolve the matter, which in and of itself is a strike against Zadok. Some have proposed that Zadok had Jebusite—that is, pre-Davidic, Jerusalemite—connections; and David brought Jebusite Zadokites into his priestly establishment as a political compromise when he took charge of the city. The ancient Near East gives numerous examples of king and priesthood uniting their respective power bases. When they do, they become a formidable entity indeed. This would partially

---

[6]To read further on the social organization of tribal and monarchic Israel, see Norman K. Gottwald, *The Tribes of Yahweh* (Maryknoll, N.Y.: Orbis Books, 1979), part 6; and Paula McNutt, *Reconstructing the Society of Ancient Israel*, Library of Ancient Israel (Louisville: Westminster John Knox Press, 1999). For an excellent discussion of the honor/shame system, see Bruce J. Malina, *The New Testament World: Insights from Cultural Anthropology*, rev. ed. (Louisville, Ky.: Westminster/John Knox Press, 1993), 28–62.

explain why it appears David took Jerusalem so easily. It would then be a simple matter to link Abiathar to that group.[7]

That would not, however, speak to the issue of Zadokite legitimacy when Abiathar was dismissed by Solomon. The Jebusites were not Yahwists and had no connection with the wilderness period and experience of ancient Israel. Nor did they have anything to do with Levi. More would be required to legitimize Solomon's choice of Zadok.

Another approach is to link Zadok with the Aaronids of Hebron. There was a tradition that Moses had an older brother Aaron: "Moses was eighty years old and Aaron eighty-three when they spoke to Pharaoh" (Exod. 7:7). That would mean that Aaron was a Levite. Chronicles lists a certain Zadok among Aaronids when David ruled from Hebron. "These are the numbers of the chiefs of those equipped for war [who] came to David at Hebron, to turn over the kingdom of Saul to him according to the command of YHWH:...from the Levites, four thousand six hundred; and Jehoiada was prince of [the house of] Aaron and with him three thousand seven hundred; and Zadok, a valiant young warrior; and from his ancestral house twenty-two officers" (1 Chron. 12:24–29).

Keepers of the Sacred Stories

We begin to see how important the role of keeper of the sacred stories was when we look at narratives about Moses and Aaron that appear in different parts of the Pentateuch. In some places Moses is presented in a leadership role; in others, Aaron is in charge.

For instance, it is to be expected that there would be a thematic pattern of humility on the part of a hero approached by God to perform a task. The initial response would be reticence on the part of the hero. "The task is too great. I do not have the ability to accomplish such a goal."

In the hands of a pro-Moses narrator, that quality of humility would be highlighted as a strength. In Numbers 12:2–3, Aaron and Miriam challenge the assumption that Moses is the primary spokesperson for God. "They said, 'Has the Lord spoken only through Moses? Has he not spoken through us also?' And the Lord heard it. Now the man Moses was very humble, more so than anyone else on

---

[7]For a readable reconstruction along these lines, see Karen Armstrong, *Jerusalem* (New York: Ballantine Books, 1997), chap. 3.

the face of the earth" (Num. 12:2–3). The narrator, in this instance, has set up the occasion for a confrontation between Aaron, Miriam, and Moses over the issue of authority to speak for YHWH. YHWH settled it by presenting Moses as the primary speaker: "He is entrusted with all my house. With him I speak face to face—clearly, not in riddles; and he beholds the form of the Lord" (Num. 12:7–8).

In the hands of a pro-Aaron narrator, the same theme of humility can take a different turn. In chapter 4 of Exodus, YHWH approaches Moses to try to convince him to go to Pharaoh and negotiate the release of the Hebrew slaves. Moses' natural reticence to take on such a formidable challenge receives continued encouragement from YHWH. YHWH insists that he will be with him in the task, but Moses persists in his refusal to accept the challenge. "O my Lord, I have never been eloquent, neither in the past nor even now that you have spoken to your servant; but I am slow of speech and slow of tongue" (Exod. 4:10). But YHWH, too, persists. "Who gives speech to mortals? Who makes them mute or deaf, seeing or blind? Is it not I, the Lord? Now go, and I will be with your mouth and teach you what you are to speak" (Exod. 4:11).

Now a pro-Moses storyteller, at this point in the story, would probably acknowledge the humility of Moses as a good quality, and then continue the narrative with Moses accepting the challenge and moving forward in spite of the risks. But not this storyteller. "But he [Moses] said, 'O my Lord, please send someone else'" (Exod. 4:13). Now the door has been opened for a new figure. "Then the anger of the Lord was kindled against Moses and he said, 'What of your brother Aaron, the Levite? I know that he can speak fluently; even now he is coming out to meet you, and when he sees you his heart will be glad. You shall speak to him and put the words in his mouth; and I will be with your mouth and with his mouth, and will teach you what you shall do. He indeed shall speak for you to the people; he shall serve as a mouth for you" (Exod. 4:14–16).

If we read this version of the presentation of Moses and Aaron from the later Zadokite perspective, after Zadok had been elevated to the position of sole high priest over the temple, it looks like a story designed to demonstrate God's choice of Zadok over the temple. It demonstrates, once again, how biblical narrative can carry multiple voices.

Solomon could dismiss Abiathar, but it is not as easy to dismiss Moses, the genealogical ancestor of Abiathar. Moses was just too central to the tradition. Still, Zadok's credentials as a Levite with ancestors connected with Israel's wilderness experience, chosen by God to speak for him, had to be established. It would need to be done in such a way that Moses' honor would be preserved, while at the same time replacing him in the primary leadership role.

Aaron was the key to such a retelling of the story, still building on the Mosaic quality of humility. In this telling of the story, Moses' reticence, while fully understandable given the enormity of the task, was held onto just a bit too long. YHWH became impatient with Moses and chose his older brother Aaron for the job. The narrative tells us YHWH knew Aaron could speak well. In the description of some of the plagues, we see that Aaron also does the miracles. Moses, in effect, in this version of the story, has been promoted upstairs—and out. He has a nice office with a wonderful view, but no duties. This sounds very similar to the Mushite Levite dilemma. It was Abiathar's problem. It was the problem of Ahijah of Shiloh in his dealing with Jeroboam I. Jeremiah was born into a priestly family in Anathoth—the place to which Abiathar was sent. But Jeremiah too was a priest with no priestly duties.

The point, here, is that the Zadokites solved the problem of family credentials by linking Zadok with Aaron, Moses' older brother. To be sure, biblical tradition often presents a younger son overshadowing an older brother to become a prominent leader, but if the social and political circumstances required it, there was always the option of reverting to the standard patriarchal system of passing the inheritance on to the older brother. David was king in Hebron, that is, in Judah, for seven years before he moved to rule over the northern tribes from Jerusalem. Hebron is remembered as an Aaronid city. If the Chronicler is correct in listing a certain Zadok from the Aaronid Levites in Hebron coming to David's support, we have a figure who is prior to the need for an Abiathar who would give voice to northern Levitical interests. Zadok now had his credentials; and with them God's blessing: "[Moses] what of your brother Aaron, the Levite? I know he can speak fluently...he shall serve as a mouth for you" (Exod. 4:13–16).

I repeat an observation made earlier about our literary-critical approach to reading the texts before us. To understand the priesthood and the spirituality of priests, we must enter into the network of relationships created by the narrative world of the storytellers. We will see that the priests' relationship to and perception of kings was part of their sense of who they were. It will often be the case that a narrative, in either Samuel/Kings or Chronicles—even though the content is focused on a king—will reflect an assessment of that king that embodies the values and spirituality of the priestly family and implied author telling the story. Fundamental to our approach is the claim that the stories about kings in Samuel/Kings and Chronicles often tell us more about priests than they tell us about kings. At the very least we are seeing the king through the lens of the storyteller.

The Priesthood in Ancient Israel

We have before us in the Old Testament at least two major priestly styles of spirituality, each with its own collection of sacred stories and each linked to the narrative tradition of a priestly family. Each family believed it was called by God to lead.

Our agenda for the next two chapters will be to examine more closely the inner dynamics of each spiritual pathway. Briefly characterized, the two modes of spirituality on opposite ends of a continuum could be described as follows: (1) A cluster of late literary strata affirms a center of meaning in Jerusalem/Zion. Within the ordered space of the temple, God consumes his sacrifice (2 Chron. 7:1–3). Believers are called to withdraw into the holy. The sacred is that which purifies. The holy embraces perfection and reaches toward higher discipline. God establishes boundaries. The sacred story moves from vulnerability to stability. The priestly family affirming this vision traced its lineage back through Zadok to Aaron. (2) An earlier cluster of literary strata affirms a center of meaning in the wilderness/Horeb. Within the wilderness, God speaks his word from a flaming mountain (Deut. 5). Believers are drawn into relationships. The sacred is that which heals. The holy embraces imperfection and reaches toward wholeness. God breaks through boundaries. The sacred story moves from slavery to freedom. The priestly family affirming this vision traced its lineage back through Abiathar to Moses.

Because there is more data about priests and Levites in later writings of the Old Testament, the movement of this book takes its clue from archaeology. Excavating a tell requires that the archaeologist begin at the top of a mound, which is the period of its latest date. As the search proceeds through the strata into the heart of the mound, one is working backward through time. Once the excavator reaches bedrock, it becomes possible to reconstruct a history of the tell, reorganizing the data into a meaningful, interpretive whole. If we adopt the metaphor of the Hebrew Bible as a stratified mound of literary data, like the archaeologist the literary critic can proceed through the literary strata backward in time, organizing the data around centers of meaning identified within the respective strata. As it becomes clearer to us where the narrative is headed, we will be on firmer ground to probe the earlier periods where the data are less and more hypotheses are required.

Our methodology will be to take sacred story seriously as a means of communicating truths about one's knowledge of the spiritual life. Our goal will be to locate a center of meaning within the various strata and from the perspective of that stance fill out the implications for understanding the spiritual life. Taken together, these literary strata form layers of meaning that give content to the national epic of ancient Israel.

2

A POLITICS OF PURITY
Aaron and Zadok

S tructural themes shaping the Aaronid Zadokite spiritual pathway are centered in a vision spatially conceived. The center of meaning is located at God's house in Jerusalem/Zion. Within the ordered space of the temple, God consumes his sacrifice (2 Chron. 7:1–3). Believers are called to draw near to the holy. The sacred is that which purifies. The holy embraces perfection, defined in terms of purity, and reaches toward higher discipline. God will not tolerate impurity; thus, God establishes boundaries. The sacred story moves from vulnerability to stability. The priestly family affirming this vision traces its lineage back through Zadok to Aaron.

To enter the social world of the Chronicler's discourse requires that the reader enter the dormant period of the exile and then the period of recovery experienced with the creation of Yehud, the Hebrew word for Judah, as a province within the Persian Empire. Yehud was the homeland, located in Palestine, for the remnant of postexilic Judah.

In 520 B.C.E. it served Darius' political agenda to offer support to Jews living in Yehud to rebuild their temple in return for stability in the region of Palestine. Darius was preparing to engage Egypt and Greece, and it would not do to have instability in Palestine. Persian policy makers had discovered that allowing conquered peoples to return to their homelands and even engage in worship of their own gods benefited the empire by extending law and order to the provinces.[1]

If we assume that Chronicles was written during the Persian period, near the date of 520 B.C.E. to celebrate the occasion of the rebuilding of the temple, we have a political setting that makes sense out of the Chronicler's discourse. The price one paid, of course, for being allowed to return to one's cultural center was that one would not seek to recover the political and military trappings of state. Rather, at that level one would assimilate into the structures of the Persian Empire and do so in a supportive way.

Aaronid Zadokite priests, because they benefited from Persian policy, could happily endorse the opportunity. Given their history of leadership in the First Temple since the days of Solomon, they had been reaffirmed in that position by the Persians. It could be argued that elites recognize other elites even among different ethnic groups. Thus, within Judaism Aaronid Zadokite priests stood at the highest level one could aspire to as a Jew in the Persian Empire. It served their interests to work toward the maintenance of law and order in the arena of their jurisdiction centered in Jerusalem. As loyal Yahwists, to be sure, they would have preferred the realization of the full vision of a restored state akin to Israel under David and Solomon.

Still, the rebuilding of the Second Temple could be the first step toward that fuller restoration. With the structures of YHWH's house now back in place and in operation, there was a context for the retelling of ancient Israel's story. There would be a renewed interest and energy in the study of the period of the First Temple because perhaps one could discern with greater clarity how it was and is that YHWH works in the world. Such a reading creates an ideal setting, then, for multiple voices seeking expression in the narrative.

---

[1] For an excellent introduction and discussion of Persia as the context for understanding early postexilic Yehud, see Jon L. Berquist, *Judaism in Persia's Shadow: A Social and Historical Approach* (Minneapolis: Fortress Press, 1995).

At one level we will be hearing the Aaronid Zadokite version of ancient Israel's story grounded in their experience of the First Temple period. In addition, the First Temple period in its entirety would also become a metaphor for lessons to be learned and applied as guidelines for steps to be taken during the Second Temple period. When was YHWH pleased in the earlier period; when was he displeased? How were these lessons to be applied within the political restraints of Yehud in the Persian period?

It is fair to ask again why, in a book about priests and priesthood, we—and the Chronicler—would choose in what follows to focus on stories about kings. Earlier on we defined spirituality as a process marked by a movement toward voice. In postexilic Yehud, to resist the colonizing pressure of the Persians in their efforts to subdue and control the identity of a conquered people required that the colonized find a space within which to tell their own story, in their own words. The rebuilding of the Second Temple was a movement toward carving out that space. But why does this mode of spirituality require such a sharp focus and intense discipline? Because this mode of spirituality was an attempt in a hostile environment to articulate publicly a counter-cultural utterance. The Persians still held the upper hand politically and militarily and could quickly remove the Second Temple space if it were perceived not to serve their interests. Aaronid Zadokite priests had to serve simultaneously their own people of Yehud and the Persian power structure.

To reach the nerve among the faithful in Yehud, who dared to hope for a national restoration, required that the narrative be cast in images alive when Israel was an independent country. The First Temple period was a time when king and priest ruled, and they did so independently. For the narrative to be "true" the stories must in some way focus on kings and kingship. The stories also had to be told in such a way that Persian "observers" would not be threatened by what they would interpret as dangerous rhetoric.

The political compromise was to permit Aaronid Zadokite priests to control the internal affairs of Second Temple life as long as it looked from the outside as if it were contained within religious practice. Purity codes defining accepted religious practice served the function of containing the energy of restoration zeal. The Aaronid Zadokites knew there were finite boundaries to what would be acceptable practice in their colonized setting. At the same time, however, they were servants of the people and believed God was acting anew in their time.

When one is in a position of political power—even if it is only partial—and can act on a vision within a concrete social space, that space shapes the content of the vision itself. Maintenance of the ritual purity of the space becomes a part of one's sense of identity and, thus, stands high on the agenda of one's spiritual journey. Aaronid Zadokite priests within the Second Temple structures of Persian Yehud grounded their vision in the narratives of David, Solomon, and First Temple Jerusalem. That narrative, in effect, became a metaphor—or formulation in terms of spiritual geography—that gave voice to the Zadokite political and religious agenda in Second Temple Yehud.

Contemporary illustrations of this mode of spirituality can be found when a community of believers commits itself to maintain and defend what is for them a holy place. They will frequently adopt a politics of purity and create clear boundaries identifying who is in and who is out.

Our goal as reader, to be faithful to the text, will be to try to hear the voice of the implied author of Chronicles.[2] If we are a Protestant Christian reader, this may mean we need to set aside for a moment, as well, a cultural bias against a sustained focus on details. Many of ancient Israel's kings have long and perhaps unfamiliar names. But this is also an instance when God is to be found in the details. How the story was told—particularly when compared to an alternate telling found in Samuel/Kings—can reveal much to us about the spirituality being followed and affirmed by the priestly family of Aaronid Zadokites during the Persian period. We aren't just dealing with neutral information about the past; these are the sacred stories of a particular social group. Their particular social situation is such that they were addressing the question of what kind of spiritual pathway could be constructed in that middle space of limited control over one's institutions. They asked, "Can one be faithful to an ancient vision rooted in the royal theology of the First Temple and still observe the political constraints imposed by the more powerful presence of the Persian empire?"

---

[2]We will seek the "plane of ultimate semantic authority," to use the language of Mikhail Bakhtin.

We will begin with the Chronicler's narrative of the divided monarchy period, since the literary units connected to the sequence of Judean kings are relatively small and thus give us time to define our terms and offer some interpretive suggestions. Then we will move— earlier in time—to the more complicated narratives about the reigns of David and Solomon in Chronicles and attempt to reconstruct the Aaronid Zadokite vision of God's activity in the world.

Kings of Judah and Israel[3]

UNITED MONARCHY		
Saul		
David (1000–961 B.C.E.)	Abiathar and Zadok	High priests
Solomon (961–922)	First Temple	Zadok as high priest
		Abiathar banished
	Civil War	
Judah (South)	DIVIDED MONARCHY	**Israel (North)**
Rehoboam –	Shishak (Egypt)	Jeroboam I
Abijah (Abijam)		Nadab
Asa		Baasha
		Elah
		Zimri
Jehoshaphat		Omri
	Elijah	Ahab
Jehoram	Elisha	Ahaziah
Ahaziah		Joram
Athaliah (Queen)		Jehu
Jehoash		Joahaz
Amaziah		Joash
Uzziah (Azariah)		Jeroboam II
Jotham (regent)		Zechariah
Jotham (king)		Shallum

[3]*Brief Notes to Chart:* (1) The abbreviation B.C.E. means Before the Common Era. (2) There was a dialectical difference in spelling in Judah and Israel that has been made consistent in the chart. It is not always consistent in the biblical text. An *h* appears in Judah and not in Israel; so Jehoash and Joash are the same name, as are Jehoram and Joram and Jehoahaz and Joahaz. (3) Note that after Ahab there is a potential for confusion in names since there was an Ahaziah and Joram/Jehoram in both Judah and Israel, though reversed. The reader needs to be sure which king is being referred to. (4) The kings of Israel are not systematically treated in Chronicles. They are discussed only if they impact the narrative about a Judean king. (5) Jehu assassinates simultaneously Ahaziah of Judah and Joram of Israel in his drive to destroy the house of Omri. Athaliah, a daughter of Ahab, married Jehoram of Judah. She too died a violent death.

	Assyria		Menahem
			Pekahiah
Ahaz			Pekah
			Hoshea
			Fall of Israel (721)
Hezekiah			
Manasseh			
Amon			
Josiah	Fall of Assyria (612)		
Jehoahaz II	Babylonia		
Jehoiakim			
Jehoiachin			
Zedekiah			
Fall of Judah (587)			
Exile (587–540)			
Yehud	Persia		
	Second Temple (520)		

Chronicles and the Aaronid Zadokite Maintenance of Purity
Rehoboam (2 Chron. 10:1—12:16)

When the reader focuses on the surface text of the Rehoboam story (2 Chron. 11:5—12:16), one encounters there a presentation of a spiritual geography expressed in narrative terms; that is, a description of an ethical norm envisioned as an ideal space with Jerusalem at the center, the abode of kings. Jerusalem is protected by fortified cities provisioned with food and weapons and commanders. Note that this particular catalogue of fortified cities (2 Chron. 11:6–10) begins with Bethlehem, David's birthplace, and ends with Hebron, the city from which David ruled for seven years over Judah. Davidic genealogies inform the selection of the king's sons dispersed among the fortified cities.

We see that priests and Levites have gathered from their common lands to Judah and Jerusalem because Jeroboam forbade them to be priests for YHWH in their own territories. Following them come more of the faithful to the land of Judah and Benjamin, for there is good in Rehoboam's land (2 Chron. 12:12). In contrast, the Deuteronomist found nothing to say that was good about Rehoboam.

The quiet was broken, however, with the arrival of Shishak invading from the south, from Eygpt. Shishak captured fortified cities and made his way as far as Jerusalem. Such an intrusion into God's holy land demanded explanation. Earlier we had heard from the narrator that when Rehoboam had become strong, he forsook the law of YHWH and all Israel with him (2 Chron. 12:1). Now we see the pattern of reporting speech is broken by reported speech—a speech that allows voice to move to a different place and/or time in the narrative world, thereby offering a different perspective—wherein the narrator quotes Shemaiah, who in turn quotes God. We learn from God's direct speech that when a people abandon God, God abandons them. Reported speech again breaks through the surface space to a previous space where, in response to God's pronouncements, we observe prince and king humbling themselves and saying, "YHWH is righteous" (2 Chron. 12:6). It is then that the tide turns in favor of Judah and Jerusalem. "I will give them a means of escape" (2 Chron. 12:7). "Nevertheless they shall become [Shishak's] servants that they may distinguish [between] my service and the service of the kingdoms of the [other] countries" (2 Chron. 12:8).

If we postulate that the voice of the implied author, controlling the speech of the narrator, was positioned within the structures of Yehud as a Persian colony, we hear a voice from a Jerusalem framed by the constraints of an occupied country, a voice searching for pattern and meaning in retelling the story of the nation's past. It was a telling, however, that sought to inform the political complexity of the author's present.

Using the literary device of reported speech, the narrator breaks through the surface of a mythic norm, informed by the royal theology still carried by the Aaronid Zadokites, into past surfaces that together reveal the complexity of compositional creation. The narrator, by retelling Rehoboam's story and his encounter with Shishak, at one level was describing a social situation of Israel under threat from Egypt. "They shall become his servants that they may distinguish [between] my service and the service of the kingdoms of the [other] countries" (2 Chron. 12:8). Shemaiah quoted YHWH, however, saying, "I shall give them some measure of escape, and my anger shall not pour out against Jerusalem" (2 Chron. 12:7–8).

This same story from an ideological stance, that is, the ultimate semantic authority of the text, may be the author affirming a position about Yehud in the Persian Empire, where now Persia represented the superior political power with which Israel must deal. To paraphrase the author's interpretive reading of the ancient text, "We have not been destroyed by Persian power. God has given us a means of escape. But we are a colony. Such a social space helps teach us to distinguish between service to YHWH and service to the powers of other countries. Yes, it is difficult. But there is good in the land. A key presence is the priests and the Levites at their duties" (2 Chron. 12:5–12).

Abijah (2 Chron. 13:1–23)

The narrator uses the platform of reporting speech to present the ethical norms that define a politics of purity. Each king is presented from the perspective of this platform. Explanations are presented with the introduction of reported speech that penetrates the surface to earlier spaces and times, offering to the reader a new perspective on an event.

Through the voice of Abijah we hear the stance of Judah toward Israel, that rebel group that broke away from the Davidic union under the misguided leadership of Jeroboam. Interestingly, northern Israel is often referred to by its earlier tribal name of Ephraim. This would work as a literary device to deny the north its identity as YHWH's Israel; that belonged to Judah. Abijah spoke from a mountain in the hill country of Ephraim. He was leading an army of 400,000 warriors, half the size of Jeroboam's 800,000: "Hear me, Jeroboam and all Israel. Is it not known to you that YHWH the God of Israel has given to David kingship over Israel forever, to him and to his sons?" (2 Chron. 13:4–5).

Rehoboam is presented as one young and indecisive when threatened by the collection of "worthless men and scoundrels" gathered around Jeroboam. But this is YHWH's kingdom, defended by sons of David, with Aaronid priests and Levites, at their duties in Jerusalem, some of whom had been banished by Jeroboam. "God is with us at our head and there are his priests and the trumpets to sound the battle cry against you. O Israelites do not fight against YHWH God of our ancestors, for you will not succeed" (2 Chron. 13:12).

Jeroboam attempted an ambush, but failed. Not only was Abijah the victor, but Bethel, that infamous northern sanctuary at which were illegitimate priests, was seized along with a few other northern towns and villages.

With this assessment of Abijah's reign the narrator introduces us to one of the major denials within the Chronicler's politics of purity:

From Jeroboam on, the Northern Kingdom of Israel did not exist. To allow even the vocabulary of its legitimacy into the narrative would begin the process of altering the identity of Judah, which saw itself as the true Israel. Living as he did in the Persian period, the author knew that the north would fall, thus confirming his assessment. The rebuilding of the temple in his day would be experiential evidence that "YHWH the God of Israel has given to David kingship over Israel forever, to him and to his sons, a covenant of salt" (2 Chron. 13:15).

To Yehud in the Persian colonial setting, the reported words by the narrator of Abijah to Jeroboam would have had a double meaning. They, of course, were part of a speech from Abijah to Jeroboam and ancient Israel; but they also held out the promise that with the rebuilding of the temple, the benefits of the eternal covenant would once again bring healing to the land and nation. "As for us, YHWH is our God, and we have not forsaken him; the priests who minister to YHWH, the sons of Aaron and the Levites, are at their duties. They make sacrifice to YHWH, burnt offerings every morning and evening, and spicy incense. They set rows of bread on the pure table. A gold lampstand and its lamps they light each evening because we are keeping the charge of YHWH our God while you [Jeroboam] have forsaken it" (2 Chron. 13:10–11).

Asa (2 Chron. 14:1—17:1)

The pattern for action by an assessed good king begins by removing false worship located at the "high places" from the land. Then one is to build fortified cities for protection. Thus can Asa claim in reported speech, "The land before us is still ours, for we have sought YHWH our God. We have sought [him] and he has given us rest on every side" (2 Chron. 14:6). Such an affirmation would clearly have resonated in the minds and hearts of Yehud's faithful. The Persians may think this is their land, but "the land before us is still ours" (2 Chron. 14:6). In times of attack, the good king relies upon YHWH; that will bring prosperity. Asa did turn to YHWH; thus, in the attack against Zerah and the Cushites all the enemy were slain, and Gerar was plundered; from the herdsmen many sheep and cattle were taken captive.

After the success, YHWH grants rest to the land, a sign indicative of God's pleasure and healing. On the basis of that gift, the good king reforms the land "putting away despicable idols" and "repairing the altar of YHWH" on which are offered acceptable sacrifices. An oath reaffirming commitment to God's covenant becomes a source of joy and renewed rest. Such rest reverses an unstable earlier time caused by lack of recognition of the true God, no teaching priest, or knowledge of Torah. "For a long time Israel had gone without the true God, without a teaching priest, and without Torah, but in their distress they turned to YHWH the God of Israel. They sought him and he was found by them" (2 Chron. 15:3–4).

With the building of the Second Temple, the environment had been created for renewed attention to reform. When Asa chose not to rely on God, he entered a period of war with Baasha, the king of Israel north of Judah. Asa made the mistake of entering into a military alliance with Ben-hadad of Syria. Rest disappeared from the land, and Asa died a man with diseased feet.

The politics of purity often draws on images and metaphors of health and disease to interpret events and make its points. Health happens when the entire system is in place and operating according to plan. Disease intervenes whenever the system is short-circuited and access to YHWH is cut off by such things as false worship at the high places, lack of a teaching priest, or a king who relies on military alliances with foreign nations rather than God. A reading of Asa's story for the faithful of Yehud would include confidence that a new era of health was at hand given the rebuilding of the temple.

Jehoshaphat (2 Chron. 17:2—21:1)

Jehoshaphat filled the requirements of a good king. He established a military presence in Judah and placed deputies in the cities of Ephraim that Asa had captured. He removed the high places and *asherim* from Judah. He sent officials, including priests and Levites, to teach from the book of the Torah. As a result, the dread of YHWH fell upon surrounding countries, convincing them not to go to war with Jehoshaphat. He received tribute from the Philistines and from the Arabs. With his wealth he built fortresses and store-cities. In addition to the warriors placed by the king in the fortified cities, he had a substantial army serving himself.

Jehoshaphat made a mistake, however, in forming a marriage alliance with Ahab of Israel. God's displeasure was voiced through the reported speech of the seer Jehu, son of Hanani, "Should one help the wicked and love those who hate YHWH? For this, wrath is upon you from YHWH. Nevertheless [some] good things have been found in you since you annihilated the asherim from the land and dedicated your heart to seek God" (2 Chron. 19:2–3).

Jehoshaphat responded to a military threat in an appropriate way. The people were prepared because from Beersheba to the hill country of Ephraim, Jehoshaphat had placed judges instructed in the Torah. The judges were to show no partiality, nor take bribes. Amariah was the chief priest over the people in all matters concerning YHWH; and the Levites were officers.

The threat came from Moab, Ammon, and Edom attacking from "beyond the sea" from Aram. Jehoshaphat appropriately went to the house of YHWH and stood in the midst of the gathered assembly of Judah and Jerusalem, including womenfolk and children. He inquired of YHWH, making reference to the building of the temple for YHWH's name, established by their ancestors.

God's response was mediated by an Asaphite singer from among the Levites in the assembly, "Do not be afraid, and do not be dismayed before this great horde, for the battle is not yours but God's...It is not for you to do battle on this [occasion]. Take your position: stand and see YHWH's deliverance of you O Judah and Jerusalem" (2 Chron. 20:15–17).

Judah came to watch the battle. There appears to have been some confusion precipitated by ambushes; since the Ammonites, Moabites, and Edomites fought among themselves, "each one helped to destroy his neighbor" (2 Chron. 20:23). It took three days for Judah to gather up all the booty. With that they returned to Jerusalem, and the kingdom of Jehoshaphat was at rest all around.

The only blemishes to Jehoshaphat's record were his alliances. An alliance with Ahaziah, successor to Ahab of Israel, brought the reported speech of Eliezer, son of Dodavahu of Mareshah: "Since you have allied yourself with Ahaziah, YHWH will destroy your work" (2 Chron. 20:37). Jehoshaphat had made ships at Ezion-geber to go to Tarshish. "The ships were wrecked and were prevented from going to Tarshish" (2 Chron. 20:37).

Lessons the narrator may have been offering from this telling of Jehoshaphat's story to the faithful of Yehud would be not to marry foreigners, which would have been an issue in the Persian period, or enter into foreign military alliances. Rather, even in the present context of provincial Persia, trust in YHWH and the institutional apparatus of the temple. This is the pathway to national health.

Jehoram (2 Chron. 21:2—22:1)

The reader anticipates right from the start that Jehoram will not be assessed as a good king. He was married to a daughter of Ahab, for which Jehoshaphat had already been admonished by Jehu, son of Hanani. The narrator lists evidence of Jehoram's "doing evil in the eyes of YHWH" (2 Chron. 21:6). He killed all his brothers, once having established himself in office. He rebuilt high places in the mountains of Judah. He led the people astray, so much so that a letter from Elijah the prophet was quoted, "YHWH will strike your people with a great plague, your children, your wives and all your possessions" (2 Chron. 21:14); and then, consistent with the use of health metaphors as language of punishment, "You yourself [will have] terrible sickness with a disorder of your bowels until your bowels come out because of the disease, day after day" (2 Chron. 21:14–15). And so it happened.

Ahaziah (2 Chron. 22:2–9)

Ahaziah didn't fare much better. His father was Jehoram. His mother was Athaliah, the daughter of Ahab, though she is referred to here as the daughter of Omri. Some have proposed the text should read "granddaughter of Omri," which would make sense. At any rate, she is in a position to advise her son as a power behind the throne, which from a purity stance could only bring disaster. "The house of Ahab became his counselors after the death of his father to his distruction" (2 Chron. 22:4).

He entered into a military alliance with Joram of Israel against Hazael of Aram. Joram was wounded in a battle at Ramah and went to Jezreel to recuperate. Ahaziah visited Joram at Jezreel only to encounter Jehu of Israel. "Ahaziah's ruin was from God, by [his] going to Joram. When he came, he went out with Joram to Jehu son of Nimshi whom YHWH had anointed to exterminate the house of Ahab" (2 Chron. 22:3). While hiding in Samaria, Ahaziah was captured and brought to Jehu, who put him to death. Athaliah used this opportunity to usurp the throne. Matters were moving from bad to worse.

Athaliah (2 Chron. 22:10—23:21)

The real hero of the Athaliah narrative is Jehoiada the priest. He had connections with the royal family in that he was married to Jehoshabeath, a sister of Ahaziah, daughter of Jehoram. When Athaliah moved to kill all the king's sons and seize the throne for herself, Jehoshabeath hid Joash, son of Ahaziah, in the house of God.

It is with the Athaliah narrative that the reader also sees developed another of the Chronicler's denials: namely, that Levites are not full-fledged priests. Or perhaps better, we see how the role of the Levite is once again co-opted into the ideology of the Chronicler. Throughout, the Levites perform a secondary role with regard to sanctity and authority. When Jehoiada decided it was time to present Joash as king, the Levites were enlisted in what perhaps was an ancient military role for them as protector of the sanctuary, defender of the king.[4] They were among the holy, so they could enter the house of YHWH. Jehoiada instructed the Levites to surround the young king with weapons in hand.

When all was ready, Joash was anointed king and all declared, "Long live the king!" When Athaliah heard the commotion, she investigated and upon discovery of what was going on, cried out, "Treachery, treachery!" Whereupon she was removed to the horse's gate of the house of the king, and they put her to death there. Similarly, they attacked the house of Baal, destroyed it, and killed Mattan, the priest of Baal.

The house of YHWH was placed under the jurisdiction of Levitical priests; gatekeepers were instructed that no one should come in who was unclean in any respect. "All the people of the land rejoiced, and the city was quiet, [once] they had put Athaliah to death by the sword" (2 Chron. 23:21).

Jehoash (2 Chron. 24:1–27)

While Jehoiada the priest lived, Jehoash ruled as a king ought to rule. According to the pattern, once the impurity that was Athaliah had been removed, the good king moved to restore proper worship at the temple. "For Athaliah, wickedness [herself] [and] her sons had broken into the house of God and had even used all the consecrated things of the house of YHWH for the Baals" (2 Chron. 24:7).

---

[4]See the interesting dissertation by Sanford L. Crossley, *The Levite as a Royal Servant During the Israelite Monarchy,* unpublished Ph.D. diss., Southwestern Baptist Theological Seminary, 1989. His thesis is: "The office of Levite became an administrative and military arm of the king. David was the key figure in the development of this role for the Levites, but it would continue throughout the period of the Israelite and Judean monarchies" (p. 3).

It was time to collect money for the temple's restoration. It fell upon the Levites to collect that tax from the inhabitants of Judah and Jerusalem. The narrator reports, however, that the Levites did not act quickly. And Jehoash had to press Jehoiada, the chief priest, to assert his authority to require the Levites to act more expeditiously. A chest was placed outside the gate of the house of YHWH. Whenever it was full, the money was brought to the king's deputies by the hand of the Levites, and in turn, artisans were hired to work on the house of YHWH. "They restored the house of God to its [former] condition and reinforced it...They were offering up burnt offerings in the house of YHWH continually all the days of Jehoiada" (2 Chron. 24:13–14).

Eventually Jehoiada grew old and died, which left Jehoash without a trustworthy mentor. After Jehoiada died, the leadership of Judah and Jerusalem forsook the house of YHWH and worshiped the *asherim* and idols, in spite of warnings from prophets. In a reported speech from Zechariah, son of Jehoiada, "Because you have forsaken YHWH, he has forsaken you" (2 Chron. 24:20). In response, they stoned Zechariah at the command of the king. The narrator observes that Jehoash did not remember the kindness of Jehoiada, but killed his son. Reported speech records an utterance from the dying Zechariah: "May YHWH see and avenge!" (2 Chron. 24:22). Immediately, the Arameans invaded Judah and Jerusalem and carried away spoil to the king of Damascus. Though the Aramean army was small, YHWH granted them success.

When they withdrew, Jehoash lay wounded. "His servants conspired against him on account of the blood of the son of Jehoiada the priest, and they slew him upon his bed. So he died" (2 Chron. 24:25). The message from the narrator to the faithful of Yehud seems clear. During the difficult days of Athaliah and the later days of Jehoash with foreign worship in the land, the one who kept Judah on the right path was the priest named Jehoiada. So now, within the context of Persian colonial rule and the presence of its foreign gods, the temple with its legitimate priests provided stability and direction.

Amaziah (2 Chron. 25:1—26:2)

The review of Amaziah is mixed: "He did what was right in the eyes of YHWH, only not with a whole heart" (2 Chron. 25:2). He slew the servants who had killed his father, and, in accordance with Deuteronomic law, he did not put their children to death. He mustered his troops in preparation for a battle against Edom. He hired mercenaries from Israel, which crossed the line. He was warned by a man of God not to enter into any negotiations with Israel, quoted in a reported speech, "O King, the army of Israel must not go with you, for YHWH is not with Israel, [not with] all those Ephraimites!" (2 Chron. 25:8).

Amaziah had been instructed to go alone. He obeyed and discharged the Ephraimites, only to have them sack cities, kill many in Judah, and seize plunder on their return home. By rejecting such dealings with Israel, Amaziah was successful in his battle against Edom. His "lack of a whole heart," though, was revealed when he returned from Edom with the gods of the Seirites: "He set them up for himself as gods; he bowed himself down before them and burned incense to them" (2 Chron. 25:14).

YHWH sent a prophet to Amaziah, who said, "Why have you looked to the gods of the people who could not deliver their [own] people from your hand?" (2 Chron. 25:15). The king rejected the warning, and we learn from the prophet's reported speech that Amaziah will be destroyed. Still confident from his victory over Edom, Amaziah pressed on by challenging Israel, and they met in battle at Beth-shemesh. Judah was overthrown by Israel, and everyone fled to their tents. Joash king of Israel captured Amaziah. He plundered Jerusalem and returned to Samaria with hostages.

Amaziah outlived Joash of Israel by fifteen years, but his turning from YHWH to the gods of Edom and his pride in challenging Israel precipitated a conspiracy against him. To avoid the confrontation, Amaziah fled from Jerusalem to Lachish, but "they sent after him to Lachish and put him to death there" (2 Chron. 25:27).

Uzziah (2 Chron. 26:3–23)

Within the politics of purity, what brings down the wrath of God is crossing a boundary intended to maintain the hierarchy of the system. As long as Uzziah filled his role appropriate to a king, he grew strong, and his fame spread even to the border of Egypt. Zechariah instructed him in the oracles of God. When all was well, Uzziah defeated enemies, fortified cities, built towers in Jerusalem, and provided food and cisterns to collect water. He was one who loved the earth.

But his very strength became his weakness when, in pride, he crossed over into a function designed for a priest, a function reserved for the sons of Aaron. He entered the sanctuary of YHWH to offer incense on the incense altar. Azariah the priest and eighty others went into the king, and a reported speech announced, "It is not for you Uzziah to offer incense to YHWH, for that [belongs] to the priests the sons of Aaron, who have been consecrated to offer incense. Get out of the holy place, for you have acted unfaithfully; moreover, there is no honor for you from YHWH God" (2 Chron. 26:18).

Uzziah was enraged and proceeded to offer incense anyway, whereupon leprosy broke out on his brow. He was rushed out of the holy place because God had struck him. Uzziah spent the rest of his days in isolation as a leper while Jotham ruled in his stead. For the faithful in Yehud living in colonial Persia, the narrator was reinforcing the message that security and stability rested on maintaining the system. In the power balance it was the priests, the sons of Aaron, who preserved access to the holy. Others, even kings, found their places appropriate to their roles.

Jotham (2 Chron. 27: 1–9)

Jotham was a strong king. He did not enter the sanctuary of YHWH as had Uzziah. He built the upper gate of the house of YHWH. He built cities in the hill country of Judah. He built citadels and towers on the wooded heights. He overpowered the Ammonites and received tribute from them in his second and third year. During the sixteen years of Jotham's reign, Uzziah remained isolated as a leper.

Ahaz (2 Chron. 28:1–27)

Ahaz lived in a difficult time, but he did not provide the leadership that would have drawn praise from the Chronicler. He made metal images for the Baals. He burned his sons in the valley of the sons of Hinnom as did foreign nations. He offered sacrifices on the high places and under verdant trees. And so YHWH allowed him to be defeated by both the Arameans and the Israelites. Pekah of Israel was particularly brutal. One hundred twenty thousand warriors of Judah were slain in a single day, including officials in the royal house. Two hundred thousand were taken as captives to Samaria.

Reported speech from the prophet Oded indicated that Israel, even acting on behalf of God, had gone too far. "See, because of the rage of YHWH God of your ancestors with Judah, he gave them into your hand; but you have killed them with a fury that touched heaven" (2 Chron. 28:9). Israel's intent had become to enslave their kinsfolk from Judah and Jerusalem, but Oded continued, "Only [are] you and they not equal in offense against YHWH your God? Now listen to me and return the captives whom you have taken away from your kinsfolk; for the fierce anger of YHWH is upon you" (2 Chron. 28:10–11). Some of the officials from Ephraim listened to Oded and ordered the captives returned. They were clothed and taken to Jericho.

Ahaz of Judah responded to the attacks from Aram and Israel by appealing for help from Assyria. This, of course, would be seen by the narrator as a military alliance evidencing a lack of trust in YHWH. As a result things got worse for Ahaz. Edom attacked. The Philistines ravaged cities in the Shephelah. The Assyrian king came not in support of Ahaz, but oppressed him further. Ahaz himself plundered the house of YHWH and the palace seeking spoil for the Assyrians in an effort to keep them away, but it did not help. Ahaz sacrificed to the gods of Damascus, closed the doors to the house of YHWH, and made altars at every corner in Jerusalem. All this only provoked the anger of YHWH all the more.

It was during these days, and the early days of Hezekiah, that Israel fell to the Assyrians. While parallels in the book of Kings go into great length seeking explanations for the fall of Israel, the Chronicler passes over the event as if it did not happen. Such a strategy is consistent with his denial that Israel ever existed in the first place.

Hezekiah (2 Chron. 29:1—32:33)

Given the length of the narrative concerning Hezekiah, it becomes clear that Hezekiah stood out as a special king in the eyes of the Chronicler. Here was a king who faced comparable challenges to those faced by those living in Persian Yehud. He inherited the internal chaos brought on by his predecessor, Ahaz, and he had to deal with the superior military threat of the Assyrians about to bring down Israel to the north, and Judah could be next. Hezekiah, however, offered the kind of leadership in such a difficult time that the Chronicler would find praiseworthy. Hezekiah was presented as one who worked within the framework of a politics of purity. He knew the value of a holy place. He recognized the political power of genealogical connection and hierarchical organization. He knew that God and the teaching of Torah needed a framework within which to work.

"In the first year of his being king, in the first month, he [Hezekiah] opened the doors of the house of YHWH and repaired them" (2 Chron. 29:3). In the politics of purity, access to God must be open. Levites were instructed to cleanse the temple of the impurities Ahaz had caused. "The priests went in to purify the innermost part of the house of YHWH. They brought out every unclean thing that they found in the temple to the court of the house of YHWH. Then Levites received [them] to carry [them] outside to the wadi Kidron" (2 Chron. 29:16). When the cleansing was completed, the appropriate sacrifices and offerings restored the service of the house of YHWH. The people rejoiced.

The passover festival was reinstated. Hezekiah set up the work rotations of the priests and Levites and reestablished the process whereby priest and Levite received food and supplies from the people. All this so that the priests and Levites might be freed up to concentrate on the Torah of YHWH. So responsive were the people that storehouses had to be built for the heaps of food and supplies. Only after the Chronicler has assured the reader that the system is back in place and functioning as it should does he move to the problem with Assyria.

The narrator presents the threat to the system in a manner consistent with the politics of purity. This time the threat was Sennacherib, king of Assyria. He encamped against the fortified cities on his way to challenge Jerusalem. Hezekiah took steps to protect the water supply. In reported speech, the king said, "Why should the kings of Assyria come and find abundant water?" (2 Chron. 32:4). Hezekiah strengthened and rebuilt broken city walls, adding another for increased protection. He appointed officers for battle. Then he spoke saying, "With us is YHWH our God to help us to fight our battles" (2 Chron. 32:8). And so the people were encouraged.

In the actual confrontation, servants of Sennacherib came up from Lachish to Jerusalem to intimidate the population into submission. The Assyrians made fun of Hezekiah's claim that "YHWH our God will deliver us from the grasp of the king of Assyria" (2 Chron. 32:11). They pointed out that Hezekiah's action would not work: "Before one altar you shall bow yourselves down and upon it you shall offer incense" (2 Chron. 32:12). What other people who had tried similar strategies had been able to stand up against the Assyrians? The Assyrians even spoke in Judahite so that those of Jerusalem sitting on the wall of the besieged city would understand the threat. They belittled the God of Jerusalem by treating YHWH "like the gods of the peoples of the earth, the work of human hands" (2 Chron. 32:19).

Hezekiah the king and Isaiah the prophet prayed, and God intervened. "YHWH sent a messenger and annihilated every mighty warrior and commander and officer in the camp of the king of Assyria" (2 Chron. 32:21), whereupon Sennacherib, the Assyrian king, returned to his home in shame and was killed by some of his own offspring. Thus, there was rest in the land, and Hezekiah was exalted in the eyes of all the nations.

Hezekiah, however, became very sick, at which time God gave him a sign. The narrator's interpretation of Hezekiah's illness was that, in pride, Hezekiah did not respond in accord with the benefits he had received from God. Therefore, the anger of God was against him, but then Hezekiah humbled himself. Thus, God's wrath did not come against Judah and Jerusalem during the days of Hezekiah. Instead, Hezekiah gained much wealth and honor and built storehouses and cities to gather his many possessions. All this overshadowed even the visit from the officials of Babylon who had come to inquire of the sign in the land when God had tested Hezekiah to see what was in his heart.

Manasseh (2 Chron. 33:1–20)

During the lengthy reign of Manasseh, successor to Hezekiah, many of the reforms Hezekiah had brought to the land were reversed. "He rebuilt the high places that Hezekiah his father had pulled down; and he set up altars to the Baalim and he made asheroth: they bowed themselves down to the host of heaven and he served them" (2 Chron. 31:3). The narrator reminds the reader in direct speech from God, "In Jerusalem my name will be forever" (2 Chron. 33:4). Again, in a reported speech to David and Solomon, "In this house and in Jerusalem which I have chosen out of all the tribes of Israel, I will place my name forever" (2 Chron. 33:7). But Manasseh was engaged in soothsaying, divination, and sorcery, and practiced necromancy and wizardry. He even set up a carved idol in the house of God.

Therefore, YHWH brought against Judah the king of Assyria, and Manasseh was taken captive to Babylon. The distress of that situation led Manasseh to humble himself before YHWH and pray to be returned to his kingdom. God heard his petition and returned Manasseh to Jerusalem. "Then Manasseh knew that YHWH was God indeed" (2 Chron. 33:13).

In response, Manasseh began to act more like a good king. He built an outer wall for the city of David. He placed officers in the fortified cities of Judah. He removed the foreign gods and the statue from the house of YHWH. Having cleansed Jerusalem, he set up the altar of YHWH and offered appropriate sacrifices. Not all was perfect, however, in that the people continued to offer sacrifices at the high places; but at least they offered the sacrifices to YHWH.

The key moment in Manasseh's career was when he humbled himself before YHWH while imprisoned in Babylon. The faithful in Yehud found themselves in similar constrained circumstances: first during the exile and now as a colony of Persia. This retelling of Manasseh's story would remind the faithful that YHWH can transform such circumstances: YHWH can transform even the evil career of Manasseh by bringing him to the point of humbling himself before the true God. The rebuilding of the temple in Yehud would have heralded a comparable national transformation, calling for humility and prayers from the people.

Amon (2 Chron. 33:21–25)

Amon was not a good king. He fell back into the earlier practices of his father, Manasseh, before Manasseh had humbled himself. "Amon did not humble himself, rather he, Amon, increased [his] guilt" (2 Chron. 33:23). His servants conspired against him and assassinated the king in his house. The people of the land intervened and struck down the conspirators and placed Josiah, the king's son, on the throne.

Josiah (2 Chron. 34:1–36:1)

Many have recognized that the twin pillars upon which postexilic life was organized were Torah and temple.[5] It is with Josiah's story that Torah assumes a central place in the Chronicles narrative.

Josiah was a good king. Even before the discovery of the book in the temple, the youthful Josiah was cleansing the land of false worship. "After purifying the land and the house, he sent Shaphan son of Azaliah, and Maaseiah the officer of the city, and Joah son of Joahaz the recorder, to repair the house of YHWH his God" (2 Chron. 34:8). Money that the Levites, guardians of the threshold, had collected was given to Hilkiah the high priest to fund the project.

---

[5]See the discussion of Torah and temple in Marcus Borg, "The Dynamics of Jewish Resistance to Rome: The Quest for Holiness," in *Conflict, Holiness, and Politics in the Teaching of Jesus* (Harrisburg, Penn.: Trinity Press International, 1984, 1998), 66–87.

While cleaning out the temple, Hilkiah found a book and reported it to Shaphan the scribe, "I have found the Book of the Torah in the house of YHWH" (2 Chron. 34:15). It was reported to the king, and thus began a reformation in earnest. The book was authenticated by Huldah, a prophetess. She reported to the king, "Thus says YHWH, 'See I am about to bring evil upon this place and upon its inhabitants, all the curses which are written in the book, that they have read before the king of Judah'" (2 Chron. 34:24). Josiah, however, was to be spared because he had been penitent and humbled himself before God when he heard the words of YHWH. He went to the house of YHWH and read publicly to the people all the words of the book of the covenant that had been found in the house of YHWH. The king stood upon his spot and committed himself to keep the demands of the covenant then moved further to cleanse the land in accord with the words of the book. "All his days they did not turn away from following YHWH the God of their ancestors" (2 Chron. 34:33).

Josiah kept the Passover. Interestingly, in a reported speech to the Levites, Josiah instructed them to "place the holy ark in the house that Solomon son of David, king of Israel, built: you need not carry it on your shoulder [any longer]" (2 Chron. 35:3). On the surface that looks like a positive step, though it does relieve the Levites of a responsibility that earlier had authenticated their authority in matters sacred. This placing of the ark within the house of God over which the sons of Aaron had ultimate charge placed the ark now under Aaronid jurisdiction.

Similarly, the reported speech, "Stand in the sanctuary according to the groupings of ancestral houses for your brothers, the common people, and let there be a share of an ancestral house for the Levites" (2 Chron. 35:5) also sounds good—unless this now institutionalized and made official the secondary status and place of Levites over against Aaronid priests. In the subsequent description of the passover sacrifice, "The priests dashed [the blood that they received] from their hand while the Levites did the flaying" (2 Chron. 35:11). The Levites are presented more than once as the group that prepared the setting; that is, they set up the preliminary requirements in anticipation of the real action performed by the priests. "No Passover like it had been kept in Israel since the days of Samuel the prophet" (2 Chron. 35:18).

Unfortunately, Josiah was killed by an Egyptian soldier as the Pharaoh Neco made his way through Israel to fight a battle at

Carchemish. Significantly, Jeremiah is mentioned as one who lamented the death of Josiah. Jeremiah was a figure closely associated with the Deuteronomistic history.

Jehoahaz (2 Chron. 36:2–4)

In rapid succession four kings are briefly mentioned with little said about them; and what is said is negative. Such brief notices not only meant they were bad kings in the eyes of the Chronicler but also supports the thesis that the Chronicler may have had among his sources the earlier Josianic edition of the Deuteronomistic history, so called Dtr1.

Jehoahaz lasted three months before the Pharaoh Neco deposed him and took him to Egypt. Neco placed Jehoahaz' brother, Jehoiakim, on the throne and laid upon the land a heavy tribute.

Jehoiakim (2 Chron. 36:5–8)

Though Jehoiakim ruled for eleven years, little is said about him other than he was bound in bronze fetters by the Babylonian Nebuchadnezzar and taken captive to Babylon.

Jehoiachin (2 Chron. 36:9–10)

Similarly, Jehoiachin lasted only three months before he, too, was taken to Babylon, captive.

Zedekiah (2 Chron. 36:11–23)

With Zedekiah we encounter again the reference to Jeremiah. Zedekiah "did not humble himself before Jeremiah the prophet [who spoke] from the mouth of YHWH" (2 Chron. 36:12). Leaders had polluted the house of YHWH. "Now YHWH the God of their ancestors had sent to them early and often through his messengers because he had compassion on his people and on his dwelling place" (2 Chron. 36:15). But they mocked, despised, and ridiculed the messengers and message "until the rage of YHWH mounted against his people to the point of no cure" (2 Chron. 36:15–16).

The Chaldeans came. "They burned the house of God, and they pulled down the wall of Jerusalem, and they burned all its palaces with fire and all its precious vessels were destroyed" (2 Chron. 36:19). Those who survived were exiled to Babylon until the rule of Persia. It was the words of Jeremiah the prophet that offered hope. All this, "to fulfill the word of Jeremiah, until the land had accepted its sabbaths. All the days of desolation it kept sabbath to fulfill [the] seventy years" (2 Chron. 36:21).

One of the functions of a Sabbath is to allow natural processes to renew a person or land that has been overextended. So, once again, the Chronicler is drawing upon a health metaphor to frame the discussion of the fall. The land needed time for the pollutants in the land to be excised, to be renewed; the land needed time to receive its Sabbaths. Then because these words of Jeremiah had been fulfilled, the occasion for this retelling of Israel's story is announced in a reported speech credited to Cyrus, the first king of Persia: "All the kingdoms of the earth, YHWH the God of heaven has given to me, and he has charged me to build for him a house in Jerusalem which is in Judah. Who among you [is] from any of this people? May YHWH his God [be] with him and let him go up" (2 Chron. 36:23). Health had returned to the land.

The Aaronid Zadokite Vision

When one is in a position of political power—even if that power is only partial—and can act on a vision within a concrete social space, that space shapes the content of the vision itself. Maintenance of the ritual purity of the space becomes part of one's sense of identity and thus stands high on the agenda of one's spiritual journey. Aaronid Zadokite priests within the Second Temple structures of Persian Yehud grounded their vision in the narrative of David, Solomon, and First Temple Jerusalem. That narrative, in effect, became a metaphor—or formulation in terms of a spiritual geography—that gave voice to the Zadokite political and religious agenda in Second Temple Yehud.

That agenda, which carried religious overtones, was to create a protected space within the colonized, therefore alien, cultural space of Persian Yehud. It was accomplished by establishing purity codes that marked a controlled access to the holy in Jerusalem, and the inhabitants of Jerusalem granted the necessary political power to monitor the boundaries. Their assessment of the kings of the First Temple period constituted a narrative expression that legitimized their political and religious actions. Their reading of God's action in First Temple Judah became normative for Second Temple Yehud.

The Spiritual Geography of the Zadokite Politics of Purity

Jerusalem as Center

For the Chronicler, it was David and Solomon, two kings of the united monarchy, who established the norm. David was the warrior. He was the one who would secure, establish, and protect God's holy city, the place where God had chosen his name to dwell forever.

Saul, David's predecessor, had failed in this responsibility as king. The Philistines turned out to be too strong. At a battle at Mount Gilboa, three of Saul's sons were slain. Saul was badly wounded and asked his armor-bearer to kill him. The armor-bearer refused, whereupon Saul killed himself. When Israelites in the valley saw that their king was dead they fled, and Philistines occupied their cities. The Philistines found Saul's body the next day, stripped it, and installed his armor in the temple of their gods. They displayed his skull in the Temple of Dagon. Out of respect for the body of the king and the bodies of his sons, the men of Jabesh-gilead carried their bodies to Jabesh, buried them, and fasted for seven days. Saul had proven unworthy of kingship, being unfaithful to YHWH, evidenced particularly by his consulting a medium.

David as Warrior

We meet David first as king at Hebron. All Israel had gathered at Hebron, where David made a covenant with them: "They anointed David as king over Israel according to the word of YHWH through Samuel" (1 Chron. 11:3).

Consistent with the internalized spiritual geography of the Zadokite Chronicler, David's first task was to take Jerusalem, occupied at that time by Jebusites. David seized the citadel of Zion and made the city his own. Joab became his military chief and commander. To illustrate the power of the Zadokite vision of a spiritual geography to shape the narrative, the Chronicler rearranged the order of data gathered from the book of Samuel, namely, the list in the narrative of David's mighty men. The Chronicler moved the list from its place in Samuel to this place in the narrative in Chronicles. To protect what is to become a holy place, one needs warriors. At the end of the list is this summary statement: "They used their strength with him in his kingdom together with all Israel to make him king, according to the word of YHWH concerning Israel" (1 Chron. 11:10). Many had gathered to David, even during the days of Saul: "Indeed day by day they kept coming to David to help him until there was a great encampment, like the encampment of God" (1 Chron. 11:23). Significant in the list of those gathered at Hebron around David the king was a "valiant young warrior" named Zadok of the house of Aaron from the Levites (1 Chron. 12:29). "All these warriors drawn up in battle array with a perfect heart, came to Hebron to make David king over all Israel; and also all the rest of Israel were of one mind to make David the king" (1 Chron. 12:39).

Gather the Priests and Levites to the City

With a king selected and Jerusalem secured, the next step was to gather the faithful, including "priests and Levites in the cities of their pasture lands" (1 Chron. 13:2). Then David said, "Let us lead the ark of God back to us since we did not seek it out in the days of Saul" (1 Chron. 13:4). The first attempt to bring the ark up from Kiriath-jearim failed. The oxen stumbled when they arrived at the threshing floor of Chidon. Uzzah—a non-Levite—reached out to steady the ark, which angered YHWH, who then struck Uzzah dead. This was enough to give David second thoughts about continuing the journey to Jerusalem, so they took the ark to the house of Obed-edom, where it remained for three months. Note that one of the rules of ritual purity will be for Levites to carry the ark.

David Established as King and Father of Sons

Meanwhile, David built a palace for himself with the help of Hiram, king of Tyre, who sent cedar wood and carpenters. David took more wives and fathered more sons and daughters. He was successful in battles against the Philistines. "So David's fame went out through all the lands as YHWH put fear of him upon all the nations" (1 Chron. 14:13).

Soon it was time to attempt bringing the ark to Jerusalem a second time; this time they would do it correctly. David established a place and pitched a tent for it. "David said that no one except the Levites should carry the ark of God; for YHWH had chosen them to carry the ark and to minister to him forever" (1 Chron. 15:2). In a reported speech to Zadok and Abiathar, the priests (one of the few references to Abiathar in Chronicles) and Levites, "Since you did not [do it] the first time, YHWH our God has broken out against us...So the priests and Levites consecrated themselves to bring up the ark of YHWH

God of Israel and the sons of the Levites carried the ark of God just as Moses had commanded; according to the word of YHWH, on their shoulders with poles upon them" (1 Chron. 15:15). Heman, Asaph, and Ethan were Levitical singers appointed to play musical instruments for the occasion. The ark was successfully brought up from the house of Obed-edom to its tent in Jerusalem amid fanfare and music. "David was leaping and dancing before YHWH" (1 Chron. 15:29), clothed in fine linen and wearing an *ephod*. Zadok was placed in charge of the tabernacle at Gibeon.

Preparations for Building a House for God

After David was established in his palace, he approached Nathan the prophet: "Here I am residing in a house of cedar, while the ark of the covenant of YHWH is under tent curtains" (1 Chron. 17:1), implying God too needs a house of cedar. Initially Nathan encouraged David, but God spoke to Nathan that evening in a vision, "Go and say to David my servant, 'Thus says YHWH: You are not the one who shall build me a house to reside [in]'" (1 Chron. 17:4). In an extended speech it became clear that God had chosen David to establish a dynasty; his son would build the temple. "When your days are fulfilled to go to your ancestors, then I will raise up your offspring after you, one of your own sons, and will establish his kingship. He will build a house for me and I will establish his throne forever" (1 Chron. 17:11–12). David was humbled by God's word and offered an extended prayer of thanksgiving: "The word which you uttered concerning your servant and concerning his house, let it stand forever, and do just as you said" (1 Chron. 17:23).

David's Job to Create Safety

In the Zadokite view of David's place in history, it was now clear that David's role was to make Jerusalem safe for the building of God's house. Therefore, he extended the kingdom by defeating many of the enemies surrounding Israel. He defeated the Philistines. He defeated Moab and exacted from them tribute. He defeated Hadadezer, king of Zobah. "When the Arameans of Damascus came to assist Hadadezer king of Zobah, David struck down twenty-two thousand men of the Arameans" (1 Chron. 18:6). The Arameans bore tribute to David. He collected gold and silver from Edom and Ammon. He placed garrisons in Edom, and they became subject to him. "YHWH made

David victorious wherever he went" (1 Chron. 18:13). When the Ammonites enlisted the support of the Arameans in an attempt to defeat David, shaming some of David's messengers by shaving their beards and exposing their nakedness, the Israelites fought against them, once again defeating the enemy. "Thus, the Arameans were unwilling to support the Ammonites any more" (1 Chron. 19:19). Such were the successes of David, even against Philistine giants.

The purpose of all this was to establish a safe place for building God's house. Stories about David's census, God's anger, and a plague administered by a divine messenger all set the occasion for the selection of the threshing floor of Ornan the Jebusite. God intervened to stop the destruction by the divine messenger who was standing at the threshing floor of Ornan the Jebusite. David said to Ornan, "Give me the place of the threshing-floor so I may build on it an altar to YHWH; give it to me at full cost, so the plague may be turned away from the people" (1 Chron. 21:21). And so it happened. This would be the place for the house of God.

David Gathers the Materials for the Building

David would not actually build the house since he had "shed much blood and fought great battles" (1 Chron. 22:3). The task of building would fall to his son and successor, Solomon. Still, because Solomon was young and inexperienced, David made many preliminary preparations. He gathered supplies and workers. He organized the hierarchy of responsibility and authority to be carried by priests and Levites. He instructed Solomon on the task that lay ahead, after which David praised YHWH for the abundance of blessings that had filled his life. "Give to Solomon my son a perfect heart to keep your commandments and your testimonies and your statutes, and to do all these things and to build the temple which I have prepared" (1 Chron. 19:19). Many sacrifices and offerings were made. Solomon was anointed king. Zadok was designated priest. Then, David "died in a good old age full of years, riches, and honor; and Solomon his son became king in his place" (1 Chron. 29:28).

Solomon and the Land

Solomon tapped into the authority of the Davidic dynasty and, at the same time, claimed the authority of God to build the temple: "Your son who shall go forth from your loins, he shall build the house for my name" (2 Chron. 6:9). If we view the narrative from the stance of the implied author and the time of the building of the Second Temple, we see a temporal connection being made between the Second and First Temples. Just as Solomon was drawing on Davidic authority, the author—likely claiming a Zadokite lineage—was drawing on the authority of Solomon, David, and God to establish his claim in his time, to speak for God.

The narrator reported a speech by Solomon: "I have arisen in place of David my father and have been enthroned on the throne of Israel just as YHWH spoke; and I built the house for the name of YHWH the God of Israel. And I have set there the ark in which is the covenant of YHWH he made with the children of Israel" (2 Chron. 6:10–11). The ark, which carried the authority of the Levites to be priests, was brought to the temple. As noted earlier, in the later narrative about Josiah, the Chronicler noted that the "burden" of carrying the ark was no longer required. Its sanctity was merged with that of the temple, transferring its oversight to the Zadokites.

The Land

Solomon then offered an extended prayer to God wherein humility before God was proclaimed to the people, and the promise of God's forgiveness was offered. Of particular interest is the reference to the land in the prayer and the place of the land in a politics of purity. One way to understand the appeal of a politics of purity is to see it as the reach for stability from a perceived stance of vulnerability. Paradoxically, a politics of purity usually represents the formulation of a theology of someone speaking from the stance of an elite class. The heroes view the world from the power position. For instance, the Chronicler's section on Solomon begins, "Solomon son of David grasped his royal power firmly and YHWH was with him and made him exceedingly great" (2 Chron. 1:1).

Historically, the author would still have felt vulnerable, since Yehud was but a colony of the Persian Empire. However, there was a window of opportunity for Yehud in that they fitted into Persia's long-range agenda. This reawakened the energy of the old Zadokite royal theology, which drives this retelling of Israel's epic narrative. New energy was drawn on to affirm three denials: (1) the Northern Kingdom from Jeroboam on did not exist; (2) the Mushite Levites were not full-fledged priests; and (3) Judah did not fall; rather, the land received the renewing energy of its seventy years of Sabbaths. The catalyst for this new burst of confidence in an old vision was the rebuilding of the temple. The land would live again.

The Call to Humility

Solomon spoke to God in his dedicatory prayer, "If they [the people] sin against you—for there is no human being who does not sin—and you are angry at them and hand them over before an enemy, and their captors take them captive to a land far or near; if they bring back to their mind in the land where they were taken captive and turn and implore compassion from you in the land of their captivity, saying…" (2 Chron. 6:36–37). Here the voice shifts from Solomon to the people to reinforce the significance of a humble stance, saying, "We have sinned; and we have acted wickedly, [and] we have become guilty" (2 Chron. 6:37). Then the voice shifts back to Solomon: "They return to you with all their heart and all their soul in the land of their captivity where they led them away captive and pray in the direction of their land which you gave to their ancestors, the city which you chose and toward the house which I built for your name, then heed from the heavens, the place of your dwelling, their prayer and their supplications, and act for their cause" (2 Chron. 6:38–39). With that, the fire of God descended from the heavens to consume the burnt offerings and sacrifices, and the glory of YHWH filled his house. The priests were unable to come near. All Israel worshiped and gave thanks.

Such a narrative would have had double meaning for the faithful in Yehud. The prayer established Solomon as the king par excellence who built the First Temple on the authority of both the Davidic dynasty and the will of God. The purity of the temple was sustained by the maintenance of humility before God as defined by Torah, such that, even if the people found themselves captive in a faraway land, if they prayed in the direction of the house that Solomon built—and for the narrator there was now the Second Temple—God would act for their cause.

Even foreigners in the land—which would be the case for Yehud—could benefit from God's grace. "If they [foreigners] come and pray toward this house, then [God] heed from heaven the place of your dwelling and do according to all the foreigner calls out to you, so that all the peoples of the earth might know your name, to fear you like your people Israel, and to know that your name is called [down] upon this house which I have built" (2 Chron. 6:33).

In this mode of spirituality, within the boundaries of the sacred, a clear hierarchy of purity was being established. Among the boundaries was the line between Aaronid Zadokite priests and Mushite Levites. In Chronicles, the Levites carried a secondary status in matters holy. Their role was to serve the priests. It is our thesis, however, that the Aaronid Zadokites with their spiritual pathway was not the only option available to ancient Israel or to Jews of the Second Temple period. The Levites also felt called by God to give voice to their vision of a spiritual pathway. It is to the Levite position that we turn in the next chapter.

3

A POLITICS OF RELATIONSHIPS
Moses and the Tribe of Levi

In the last chapter, we suggested that in spite of the focus on what looked like a history of the Judean kings, the implied author of Chronicles constructed the narrative in such a way that, in the assessment of the kings of Judah, we were really learning about the values and worldview of Aaronid Zadokite priests. We weren't just dealing with neutral information about the past. These were sacred stories of a particular social group, and their social situation was such that they were addressing the question: What kind of spiritual pathway could be constructed in that middle space of limited control over one's institutions? Could one be faithful to an ancient vision rooted in the royal theology of the First Temple and still observe the political constraints imposed by the more powerful presence of the Persian Empire?

Their solution was to create a protected space within the colonized—therefore, alien—cultural space of Persian Yehud. That was accomplished by establishing purity codes that marked a controlled access to the holy in Jerusalem. They were granted the necessary political power to monitor the boundaries. Their assessment of the kings of the First Temple period constituted a narrative expression that legitimized their political and religious actions. Their reading of God's action in First Temple Judah became normative for Second Temple Yehud.

Mushite Levite Discourse

Moving to the narrative in Samuel/Kings about First Temple Judah and Israel, our claim is that we shift to a Mushite Levite discourse. To pick up the story where we left off in chapter 1, after the firing of Abiathar by Solomon and Jeroboam I's rebuff of Ahijah of Shiloh, the priestly family of Mushite Levites was once again forced into a wilderness experience; they were being silenced by those who held political power. Their challenge would be: Could they experience and give voice to the hand of God in the turn of events they had to face? Is there a discernible spiritual pathway that is at home in the wilderness when one is faced with what feels like the absence of God?

We noted that, when compared with Chronicles, the narrative in Kings reflected a different social space. It is with the figure of Abiathar and the Mushite Levites that we have a window into a voice from the margins of ancient Israelite life. To be sure, that voice needs to be reconstructed. We will argue that they did indeed construct their spiritual pathway by humanizing the narrative, naming the powers, and redefining the holy in terms of healing—all of which are characteristics of the Deuteronomistic narrative. It is true that the narrative has been written over by the dominant voice coming from Jerusalem in Solomon's day, but the authority of Moses and David in tradition have assured that they were not silenced completely.

Using the list of characteristics summarizing Aaronid Zadokite spirituality offered in chapter 2 for comparison, we propose an alternate mode of spirituality, which also has a tradition in the Hebrew Bible. An earlier cluster of literary strata, when compared with Chronicles, affirms a center of meaning in the wilderness/Horeb. Within the wilderness, God speaks his word from a flaming mountain (Deut. 5). Believers are drawn into relationships. The sacred is that which heals. The holy embraces imperfection and reaches toward wholeness. God breaks through boundaries. The sacred story moves from slavery to freedom. The priestly family affirming this vision traced its lineage back through Abiathar to Moses.

Our point of entry into a closer examination of this mode of spirituality will begin with the Elijah narrative, because these stories reintroduce the central theme of the wilderness experience. To keep the names of the kings straight, it will be helpful to offer again the king list, which summarizes their relative position to one another.

Kings of Judah and Israel[1]

	UNITED MONARCHY	
Saul		
David (1000–961 B.C.E.)	Abiathar and Zadok	High priests
Solomon (961–922)	First Temple	Zadok as high priest
		Abiathar banished
	Civil War	
Judah (South)	**DIVIDED MONARCHY**	**Israel (North)**
Rehoboam	Shishak (Egypt)	Jeroboam I
Abijah (Abijam)		Nadab
Asa		Baasha
		Elah
		Zimri
Jehoshaphat		Omri
	Elijah	Ahab
Jehoram	Elisha	Ahaziah
Ahaziah		Joram
Athaliah (Queen)		Jehu
Jehoash		Joahaz
Amaziah		Joash
Uzziah (Azariah)		Jeroboam II
Jotham (regent)		Zechariah
Jotham (king)		Shallum

---

[1]*Brief Notes to Chart:* (1) The abbreviation B.C.E. means Before the Common Era. (2) There was a dialectical difference in spelling in Judah and Israel that has been made consistent in the chart. It is not always consistent in the biblical text. An *h* appears in Judah and not in Israel; so Jehoash and Joash are the same name, as are Jehoram and Joram, Jehoahaz and Joahaz. (3) Note that after Ahab there is a potential for confusion in names since there was an Ahaziah and Joram/Jehoram in both Judah and Israel, though reversed. The reader needs to be sure which king is being referred to. (4) The kings of Israel are not systematically treated in Chronicles. They are discussed only if they impact the narrative about a Judean king. (5) Jehu assassinates simultaneously Ahaziah of Judah and Joram of Israel in his drive to destroy the house of Omri. Athaliah, a daughter of Ahab, married Jehoram of Judah. She too died a violent death.

	Assyria	
		Menahem
		Pekahiah
Ahaz		Pekah
		Hoshea
		Fall of Israel (721)
Hezekiah		
Manasseh		
Amon		
Josiah	Fall of Assyria (612)	
Jehoahaz II	Babylonia	
Jehoiakim		
Jehoiachin		
Zedekiah		
Fall of Judah (587)		
Exile (587–540)		
Yehud	Persia	
	Second Temple (520)	

Elijah

"Now Elijah the Tishbite from Tishbe of Gilead, said to Ahab, 'As YHWH the God of Israel lives, before whom I stand, there shall be no dew or rain these years except by my word!'" (1 Kgs. 17:1).

Immediately obvious to the reader of the King's presentation of the divided monarchy is the inclusion of the material from the Elijah–Elisha cycle and the fact that the Deuteronomist includes the kings from both Israel and Judah. Following Polzin's observation that the fall of Eli's priestly house was a parabolic announcement early on of what would eventually happen to the royal houses of both Israel and Judah,[2] we see the split of the kingdom as the beginning of a fracture that will bring the fall to completion: first, in Israel to the north then in Judah to the south. The violence of the Jehu revolution against the house of Omri, which simultaneously eliminated Joram of Israel and Ahaziah of Judah, was an extension of the collapse leaving Judah open to Athaliah, also of the house of Omri. In time she too would be killed.

The symmetry of the Deuteronomist's presentation of the kings' annals, structured by formulaic patterns as they were, was broken by

---

[2]Robert Polzin, *Samuel and the Deuteronomist. A Literary Study of the Deuteronomic History: Part 2, 1 Samuel* (San Francisco: Harper & Row, 1989), 44.

the Elijah–Elisha materials. The narratives expanded considerably the information we have about Ahab and others of the Omrid dynasty. It looks like an intrusion of material redacted secondarily into the book of Kings. Yet the literary formulation itself is indicative of the wilderness themes that come to the fore with the Elijah stories. What was orderly and structured took on new form; old boundaries were being broken to make room for a new voice. Ahab, in effect, had become a new Solomon in the arbitrariness with which he exercised power; and Elijah emerges as a Moses figure from the wilderness to challenge Ahab's policies.

All of this sounds like a discourse that would be quite at home within Mushite Levite tradition. After Solomon dismissed Abiathar, we hear no more from Abiathar; his voice was silenced. Unless, however, and this is our proposal, the priestly family he represented— the northern Levites who traced their lineage to Moses—stands behind as one of the support groups for the entire Deuteronomistic history. Their prophetic voice would no longer come from the Jerusalem temple, but it would be reflected in the appearance of Ahijah of Shiloh and Jeremiah from Anathoth. It would not be difficult to imagine Mushite Levite priests supportive of Elijah against Ahab.

In addition, if we work with the hypothesis that Jeremiah in conjunction with Baruch, his scribe, were the implied authors/editors of this material,[3] we have a voice connection between Jeremiah and Elijah, both figures who embodied values of Mushite Levite tradition. Jeremiah had been born into a priestly family at Anathoth. That is the city to which Solomon exiled Abiathar. Also, by setting up a voice path between Elijah and Ahab, Jeremiah was reaching back through time to the days when Ahab was king in the north, in Israel. With the simple mention of those two names, Elijah and Ahab, there would have been echoes reaching far into the past, carrying meaning for the hearers, who would have known the Mushite Levite story.

With Elijah there are echoes that reach back to the time of Moses in the wilderness, a place of origin. We recall Moses standing before the flaming mountain of God receiving and voicing the word of God in the presence of what was to become Israel. "I will raise up for them a prophet like you [Moses] from among their own people; I will put my words in the mouth of the prophet, who shall speak to them

---

[3]See Richard Elliott Friedman, *Who Wrote the Bible?* 2d ed. (New York: Harper & Row, 1990), chap. 7.

everything that I command" (Deut. 18:18). Each generation would have its spokesperson to link their present with the ancient past. Jeremiah and Elijah stand in that tradition.

Ahab was a new Solomon who bore all the negative memories associated with Solomon within the Mushite Levite story. Abiathar had been dismissed from his priestly role. The hope once held out toward Jeroboam I by such leaders as Ahijah of Shiloh was dashed when Jeroboam "made priests from among the people who were not from the Levites" (1 Kgs. 12:31). "Even after this incident Jeroboam did not turn from his evil way, but he went on and made priests for the high places from among the people; anyone who desired, he ordained as priests for the high places" (1 Kgs. 13:33). This practice became sin to the house of Jeroboam (1 Kgs. 13:34).

Under Ahab and his wife Jezebel, a faithful Canaanite woman, Yahwism was threatened during the time of Elijah. It was a time calling for a word from God. Into that stance came Elijah, declaring the drought was God's will, a situation that would not change until God had spoken his word through Elijah. The narrator had created a narrative world into which was built a tension calling for healing. By implication, that same healing was being sought by Jeremiah during the last days of Judah.

God to Elijah

To become an agent for healing requires that one become familiar with desolate places; indeed, one must learn to draw nourishment from the desolate places. God spoke to Elijah: "Turn east to hide yourself by the Wadi Cherith" (1 Kgs. 17:3). There Elijah was to drink water from the wadi, a place where ravens would nourish him with bread and meat, morning and evening.

A desolate place is a place where it appears that God is absent. Someone must go into that place carrying a word to bring waters that nourish. But desolate places take their toll. Before Elijah would be ready to engage the likes of Ahab and Jezebel, he would first need to learn by experience that the desert places can also nourish. There is water in the wadi; there are ravens to bring bread and meat, morning and evening.

Wadis and ravens in the hands of the narrator became metaphors for those desolate places to which we are called, places where only we are positioned to speak the life-giving word. They stretch us beyond our current levels of comfort. The narrative describes a process wherein prayer and preparation for healing require that the boundary of our horizon relax into a larger order; that our eyes grow accustomed to the dark; that we listen for sounds in silent places; that we recognize the ravens when they bring bread and meat; that we find the wadis that provide water to drink. In the desert places our spiritual capacity deepens in preparation for healing actions.

Then one day, "The water in the wadi dried up because there was no rain in the land" (1 Kgs. 17:7). The voice of God returned again to Elijah, this time directing him toward another desolate place. Only this time it was a place of social desolation. Elijah was sent to Zarephath, which belonged to Sidon, a city in Phoenicia. Not only was Elijah now an alien in a foreign land, but he was sent to a widow-woman living with her young son. Socially a widow in the ancient Near East was in a very vulnerable position. She must survive without some man looking after her interests. This widow's vulnerability was accentuated by the lack of food caused by the drought that was taking over the land. Elijah had crossed a number of social boundaries to engage this widow-woman in conversation. We know, however, from Mushite Levite tradition that there is a special interest in widows, orphans, and aliens and their plight in Israel's social system.

Here, too, however, Elijah must learn to find resources where one would not expect them. The widow was gathering twigs to bake a small cake for her son and herself so "that we may eat it and die" (1 Kgs. 17:12). The times were desperate. Deserts, both physical and social, were linked in the narrative. To bring healing, once again Elijah must let the horizons of his spirituality expand to include the desolate places manifest in social situations. He asked for nourishment that she was to provide, and—just as the wadi provided drink and ravens brought bread and meat morning and evening—the woman's jar of meal and jug of oil did not fail them. "She ate, he and she, and her household [for many] days" (1 Kgs. 17:15).

Without overromanticizing the narrative, is it not so that when we find ourselves lacking the material resources we would wish, we reach a little deeper by asking to discover spiritual reservoirs from which we may draw on food that nourishes deeper regions of our being? The jar of meal and the jug of oil do not fail us. Elijah, the alien in a foreign land, and the widow-woman found a way, in his asking, to be responsive to a word spoken by YHWH through Elijah.

So now, once again, the "water in the wadi dried up because there was no rain in the land." Only this time it was the widow-woman's son. He grew deathly ill: "His sickness was so strong there was no breath left in him," (1 Kgs. 17:17). Of course, the woman was devastated: "What have you against us, O man of God."

Elijah took the boy "to the upper chamber where he was staying and he laid him down upon his bed" (1 Kgs. 17:19). Elijah, too, was reaching beyond his understanding as he turned to God in prayer. "YHWH my God have you brought evil upon the widow with whom I am staying by causing the death of her son?" He stretched himself upon the child three times and called upon God, "YHWH my God, please let the life of this child come back into him again" (1 Kgs. 17:21).

What are we to make of this turn of events? Remember that Elijah was directed into a desolate place two times over: first, by the Wadi Cherith; and second, to the house of the widow-woman in Zarephath, in a foreign land. Had Elijah learned his lessons? Had he learned that there are resources for healing in desolate places; there are wadis that bring drink; there are ravens who bring bread and meat; there are jars of meal and jugs of oil that do not fail us? Could Elijah find their nourishment now?

In the desolate place to which Elijah had been sent what did he do? Notice it was an action. He gathered himself around the boy and took him upstairs to his room, laid him on his bed, stretched himself upon the child three times, and prayed beyond his understanding. The text does not say that God explained to Elijah why all this was happening. Elijah was simply to be there, an alien in a widow's home, directing his voice to God in prayer: "YHWH my God, let the life of this child come back into him again."

We are the eyes and heart, the ears and mouth, the hands and feet of God in this world. There is an energy flow that connects us all to God, an energy flow that heals our wounds and hurts, even those in the deep and dark places. To be sure, one day our bodies will give way to the dust of the earth from which they came. But, miracle of miracles, the breath of life blown into our form at creation is eternal. It responds to prayer. Its energy can be fed by ravens in the desert, by the jar of meal and the jug of oil that doesn't fail.

The text tells us that Elijah returned the boy to his mother and said, "See, your son lives." Elijah's role was simply to be there, a channel through whom God could work. He didn't understand the whys and hows of the events he experienced. In many respects he was living beyond himself. Because he began the process of becoming familiar with the desolate places, he was positioned to become an agent for healing.

Elijah and Ahab

Elijah was now ready to confront the political wilderness in place because of the rule of Ahab and Jezebel. Once again, in an unexpected place, Elijah found a resource: Obadiah was in charge of Ahab's house. In that wilderness Obadiah was a protector of Yahwistic prophets. Like the ravens and the widow, he hid them away and nourished them with bread and water.

The drought and famine pressed on, forcing even Ahab to search for water and grass for his animals. Elijah found Obadiah and asked that he announce his presence to Ahab. Although Obadiah was afraid that Elijah might disappear, he agreed. Ultimately, this led to a confrontation between Elijah and the prophets of Baal and Asherah. Appropriately for Mushite Levite tradition, the contest took place on a mountain. Fire consumed Elijah's sacrifice, and there was heavy rain.

The theme of wilderness experience remanifested itself in Elijah's subsequent fear and flight from Jezebel, who moved to avenge the death of her prophets. Elijah returned to center within Mushite tradition, namely, to the mountain in the wilderness called Horeb. There he hid in a cave. Wind, earthquake, and fire manifested, but YHWH was not in them. Rather, YHWH appeared to Elijah in a still, small sound: "What are you doing here Elijah?" (1 Kgs. 19:13). Go, return. Anoint Hazael over Syria; anoint Jehu over Israel; and anoint Elisha as your successor. The YHWH of Mushite tradition was deeply involved in political affairs, actively seeking to create structures of justice. Elijah was not the only faithful servant of YHWH: "I will leave seven thousand in Israel, all the knees that have not bowed down to Baal and every mouth that has not kissed him" (1 Kgs. 19:18). The wilderness of Elijah's arrogance was balanced by the still, small sound of YHWH's call to return to the tasks at hand. The power of chaos is that it will take charge of our responses to events, causing us to withdraw in fear. The creative act reverses that process by engaging the powers. One resumes action in the name of YHWH.

Naboth's Vineyard

The writer of the Deuteronomistic history is deeply familiar with the social interaction of those in positions of power manipulating, through war, the structures of society. Caught up in the political turmoil is the voice of the narrator seeking to keep the readers' focus on the hand of God moving through potentially chaotic events. Themes of healing and justice recur throughout the stories. Often the stories are told from the perspective of the marginalized.

We learn of Ben-hadad of Aram besieging Samaria, clearly with the upper hand. Yet in the midst of that public place we hear the voice of God voiced through "a certain prophet": "Thus says YHWH, 'Have your seen all this great horde? I will give it into your hands today and you shall know that I am YHWH'" (1 Kgs. 20:13).

Ahab was successful in battle against Ben-hadad that day but made the mistake of violating rules of holy war: He freed Ben-hadad and made a treaty with him. "Since you have let the man go whom I had banned, it will be your life for his life and your people for his people" (1 Kgs. 20:42). Ahab set out for his house sullen and dejected.

We hear echoed in the story of Naboth's vineyard (1 Kgs. 21:1–19) a theme consistent with the Mushite Levites' experience with those in power. As in Abiathar's case, Ahab acted arbitrarily. He sought to acquire Naboth's vineyard, even though initially offering Naboth money or different land. But within this collection of stories there is a strong sense of God's will established in tradition that cannot be dismissed arbitrarily by those who may be powerful. Naboth said to Ahab, "May YHWH forbid that I should give you my ancestral inheritance" (1 Kgs. 21:3).

To be sure, Jezebel intervened and removed Naboth as a problem, but the narrative is clear: "Have you murdered and taken possession...I am here to bring disaster on you" (1 Kgs. 21:21). The narrator recalls what happened to the house of Jeroboam and the house of Baasha. Justice will prevail.

It is our contention that the Mushite Levite family of priests—though officially silenced—stands in the support group making sure that stories like this survived. Abiathar over against Solomon, Ahijah of Shiloh over against Jeroboam I, and Elijah against Ahab all would give the priest/prophet Jeremiah courage to affirm with Naboth over against the likes of Jehoiakim: "May YHWH forbid that I should give you my ancestral inheritance." In this instance that inheritance is the right to speak God's will, a right that extended back to Moses of the tribe of Levi.

Naming the Powers

The Micaiah narrative permits us to name the powers. It is frequently those in a marginalized social space who are much more sensitive to issues of power in a social system. Because they have to maneuver around and among those more powerful than they, they must create a mental picture of the terrain, as it were, in order to survive. Where is the danger? Where are the sources of hope?

It is with the Micaiah narrative that we see a fuller presentation of the geography of the universe. In a vision, Micaiah "saw YHWH sitting on his throne, and the whole host of heaven standing about him on his right and on his left" (1 Kgs. 22:19). Micaiah was affirming that this is the place where events are decided, not in Ahab's palace in Samaria. Spirits in YHWH's divine council debated among themselves on how to remove Ahab from kingship over Israel. YHWH stands as the ultimate arbiter among the proposals offered. "One spirit came forward and stood before YHWH and said, 'I will entice him.' YHWH said to it, 'By what means?' It said, 'I shall go forth and be a spirit of deception in the mouth of all his prophets.' And he said, 'You shall entice him and you shall succeed. Go forth and do it'" (1 Kgs. 22:21–22).

This, then, became the will of God to be voiced by the prophet amid the political events being addressed. Ahab and Jehoshaphat were seated at the city gate of Samaria inquiring of the prophets about whether to go to war against Aram at Ramoth-gilead. Many said yes, including Zedekiah, son of Chenaanah.

But after Micaiah had described his vision he said, "Now see, YHWH has put a spirit of deception in the mouth of your prophets, and YHWH has spoken evil about you" (1 Kgs. 22:23). Whereupon Zedekiah struck Micaiah on the cheek and said, "Which way did the spirit of YHWH pass from me to speak to you?" (1 Kgs. 22:24). Micaiah was imprisoned to await the actual turn of events.

When compared with the narrative in Chronicles, the source of voice in Samuel/Kings is much more often found among the marginalized. It is servants who speak, offering advice even to kings. Widows in conflict with creditors seek help. In an Elisha narrative, once again, oil did not fail as Elisha told the woman, "Go, sell the oil and you shall pay your debt, and you [and] your children shall live off the rest" (2 Kgs. 4:70). A Shunammite woman bore a son in old age, but he died while working in a field with his father. Then, as with

Elijah, "Elisha came to the house and there was the boy dead, lying on his bed. So he went in and closed the door behind the two of them and he prayed to YHWH...and then the boy opened his eyes" (2 Kgs. 4:32). Reminiscent of later Jesus stories, Elisha feeds hundreds during a time of famine, with but a little bread and vegetables. "They ate and left some remaining" (2 Kgs. 4:43–44). Lepers were healed. A workman's tool was rescued. A widow recovered lost land. It is clear that the Elijah–Elisha cycle stands in the liberation tradition of Moses and the exodus, a tradition Mushite Levite priests would continue to affirm in spite of the "sin of Jeroboam."

Violence in the Deuteronomistic Narratives

For Mushite Levite priests, the house of Omri and all those connected with him were clearly the wrong path. Particularly bad was Ahab in Israel and Athaliah in Judah. It would fall to Jehu of Israel to purge the north, and the priest Jehoiada to purge the south. Jehoiada would enlist the support of the Carites and the royal guard. After Athaliah's assassination, "Jehoiada made a covenant between YHWH and the king and the people that they should be a people to YHWH, and between the king and the people" (2 Kgs. 11:13). Within the Deuteronomistic worldview any worship of Canaanite deities was unacceptable.

After the death of Jehoiada things did not go well for Judah. Jehoash ordered that money collected at the temple be used for its restoration. Apparently, however, the priests in charge did not fulfill this responsibility. "By the twenty-third year of King Jehoash the priests [still] had not repaired the dilapidation of the house" (2 Kgs. 12:7). They were relieved of the responsibility, and money collected was given directly to the workers. Once again, in this collection of stories it was the common person who was trusted: "They did not audit the men into whose hands they had put the money to be given to those doing the work, for they were acting uprightly" (2 Kgs. 12:16).

Events turned for the worse, however, when Hazael invaded even into the land of Judah. Jehoash collected money from consecrated things and gold from the treasury "and sent [them] to Hazael king of Aram [who] then went away from Jerusalem" (2 Kgs. 12:19). That was enough to convince some within Judah that YHWH was displeased with Jehoash. A group of conspirators arose against Jehoash of Judah, and the king was struck down.

The violence of the Jehu and Athaliah narratives is not attractive. The description of Jezebel's demise is particularly gruesome. This raises the question for us the readers, In what way can these themes of violence be integrated with the themes of compassion and healing directed toward vulnerable ones so obvious in the Deuteronomistic history? Perhaps we are to read the violence as part of the wilderness experience itself. Elijah's fear and arrogance in his flight from Jezebel to Horeb can take on a life of its own and become a massacre and vengeance in the hands of Jehu. The narrator's voice enters the world of violence and becomes part of the experience of God's absence. Compassion is swallowed up in a frenzy. War is affirmed as holy. But the narrator, too, seems to be struggling with the accomplishments of Jehu. YHWH said to Jehu, "Because you have acted well in doing the right thing in my eyes, and according to all that was in my heart you have done to this house of Ahab, your sons to the fourth generation shall sit on the throne of Israel" (2 Kgs. 10:30). "But Jehu did not take care to walk in the Torah of YHWH the God of Israel, with all his heart; he did not turn aside from the sins of Jeroboam that he caused Israel to sin" (2 Kgs. 10:31). Jehu still didn't recognize the leadership role the Mushite Levites felt called to fulfill.

Similarly, Jehoash was caught up in the events that led to the assassination of Athaliah orchestrated by Jehoiada the priest. "While Jehoiada the priest instructed him" he did well, but after the priest died, Judah faced the pressure from the Syrians, which ultimately led to the assassination of Jehoash. To be sure, there are times when the instruments of power must be used to realize God's will against evil; but the tellers of these stories seem also to be aware that power—even in the hands of the faithful—can take on a life of its own and corrupt.

Assyria

With Ahaz, the narrative has reached a new level of intensity. It is now not simply a matter of a priest losing his job or even a king abusing his power with arbitrary actions. It is not a matter of bad weather putting a strain on the productivity of the economic system. Israel's existence was at stake.

Assyria was at the border and threatening both Israel and Judah. Ahaz and his successors were dealing with issues of national identity and survival. After Zechariah in the north, the fourth generation in dynastic succession after Jehu came to an end. Political order quickly fell apart. Shallum killed Zechariah; Menahem killed Shallum; Pekahiah did succeed his father Menahem; but Pekah killed Pekahiah; and Hoshea killed Pekah. During Hoshea's reign, Israel fell to Assyria. Samaria became a province of the Assyrian Empire. Israel was gone.

What were the options for healing now that the political environment had become so chaotic? Kings tried to appease the invaders by offering tribute to buy them off. Ahaz of Judah did buy himself time with that strategy. Ahaz even rearranged temple structures in Jerusalem on Assyrian models after he had visited Damascus, now in Assyrian control.

Assyrian military policy in dealing with conquered peoples was to transplant populations. Evidence of YHWH's displeasure, expressed by the Deuteronomist, was the narrator's observation, "It happened at the beginning of their settling there [in Israel] that they did not reverence YHWH, so YHWH sent lions against them which were killing them" (2 Kgs. 17:25). The people complained to the king of Assyria. Interesting was the call, voiced by the king of Assyria himself, for the wisdom of the teaching priests: "Send there one of the priests whom you exiled from there, that they may go and dwell there and he will teach them the way of the god of the land" (2 Kgs. 17:27). "And so one of the priests whom they exiled from Samaria came and dwelt in Bethel and he taught them how they should reverence YHWH" (2 Kgs. 17:28). The content for a solution for problems in the land was to return to the demands of the covenant voiced by YHWH at Horeb. "You shall reverence only YHWH who brought you up from the land of Egypt with great power, and with outstretched arm, to him you shall bow yourselves down, and to him you shall sacrifice" (2 Kgs. 17:36). But they did not listen; they simply went on acting according to their former ways.

Hezekiah

The confrontation with Assyria reached a climax during the reign of Hezekiah. The turbulence of the encounter is reflected in the vigor of the speeches exchanged at Jerusalem's wall. The Rabshakeh challenged the authority of YHWH in the presence of the people, as an audience seated on the wall. Isaiah voiced YHWH's response that God would defend his city Jerusalem. Hezekiah is presented in the Deuteronomistic narrative as one of the few kings who did what was right in the eyes of YHWH. He listened to Isaiah the prophet, who spoke for YHWH in this generation (Deut. 18:18).

What is to be noticed too is that the threat from Assyria was worked out within the politics of relationships. In the public space outside Jerusalem's wall the Rabshakeh, Isaiah, and Hezekiah were presented as the principal characters, with YHWH shaping the events. The presentation of Hezekiah in the book of Kings was essentially a Davidic vision modified by a Mosaic one. The Davidic voice came from Isaiah.

The Mushite Levites would have supported this stance because of their fondness for David, who had befriended their Levitical ancestor Abiathar. In Hezekiah's day, refugees from the Assyrian takeover of Samaria—among them, Mushite Levites—found in Hezekiah one who welcomed them, offering safety in a violent time. They could say with integrity that "he [Hezekiah] held firmly to YHWH; he did not turn away from him but kept his commandments that YHWH had commanded Moses" (2 Kgs. 18:6). Similarly, Isaiah's deeply held belief that Jerusalem would not fall was rooted in the Davidic royal theology. Therefore, Isaiah could with equal integrity affirm that "He [Hezekiah] did what was right in the eyes of YHWH according to all that David his [fore]father had done" (2 Kgs. 18:3). Isaiah affirmed for YHWH, "I will defend this city to save it for my own sake and for the sake of David my servant" (2 Kgs. 19:34).

The bridge that needed to be built in the narrative about Hezekiah was a bridge that linked the Davidic vision of safety at Zion with the Mosaic vision of freedom in the wilderness. Perhaps some of this pressure came from an exilic edition of the Deuteronomistic history, ultimately an edition that had to struggle with the fall of Jerusalem. The royal theology depended on an interventionist theology, and to be sure, during Hezekiah's day it did appear that YHWH did intervene when the Assyrians withdrew.

But a visit from Babylon by Berodach-baladan prefigured trouble to come for Judah. Isaiah voiced YHWH's judgment, though Hezekiah acknowledged, at least for now, "Will there not be peace and security in my days?" (2 Kgs. 20:19). It would be the Mosaic vision—precisely because it was rooted in a wilderness experience—that would provide a deeper spiritual pathway to deal with what was to come.

Josiah

The bridge to the Mosaic vision was accomplished with the Deuteronomistic presentation of Josiah. In detail after detail "there had been no king like him who turned to YHWH with all his heart, with all his being, and with all his might according to all the Torah of Moses" (2 Kgs. 23:25). The inspiration for Josiah's actions came from the discovery of a book in the temple, a book thought by many scholars to be a portion of what we now know as Deuteronomy. As such it embodied the values of the Northern Kingdom, values the Mushite Levites would certainly have supported. Josiah ordered the reformation of many religious practices in the south. He reinstituted the celebration of the Passover, the central festival of the Moses tradition. Comparing names listed in the Josiah narrative of the book of Kings with names in the book of Jeremiah, it could be argued that Josiah was even open to hiring priests in Jerusalem with Mushite Levite credentials. After the death of Josiah, when the tide turned against the Mushite tradition, it still appears that Jeremiah—now a peripheral priest/prophet—had protectors in high places. Much of the evidence points to the writing of a first edition of the Deuteronomistic history during the reign of Josiah in celebration of the transformations he instituted. Finally, Judah had a king Mushite Levites could fully support. The fall of Nineveh, the capital of Assyria, in 612 would have been read as confirmation of YHWH's pleasure with Josiah and his policies.

All of this came to a screeching halt in 609 when Josiah was killed. "In his days, Pharaoh Neco of Egypt went up to the king of Assyria at the river Euphrates, and King Josiah went to meet him and he [Pharaoh Neco] killed him at Megiddo when he saw him" (2 Kgs. 23:29). The best the Deuteronomist can do for an explanation for why God would allow this to happen was to blame a predecessor of Josiah, namely, Manasseh. "YHWH did not turn from the fierceness of his great wrath whereby his wrath was kindled against Judah on account of all the provocations with which Manasseh had provoked him" (2 Kgs. 23:27).

All the good actions of Josiah could not stem the tide. YHWH said, "I will remove Judah also from before me as I have removed Israel, and I will cut off this city that I have chosen, Jerusalem and the house of which I said, 'My name shall be there'" (2 Kgs. 23:27). It was clear that a spiritual pathway capable of dealing with the terrain of the wilderness experience would be needed for what lay ahead. This had been, and now once again would be, the experience of the Mushite Levite priestly family.

Jehoiachin

Moving ahead through the narratives about Jehoahaz, Jehoiakim, Jehoiachin, and Zedekiah to the last scene in the Deuteronomistic history, we read that Jehoiachin had been imprisoned for thirty-seven years. Then the text says he was released to eat in an honored setting with Evil-merodach, king of Babylon. "So he [Jehoiachin] changed his prison garments and ate bread regularly before him all the days of his life. As for his allowance, a regular allowance was given him by the king, a portion day by day all the days of his life" (2 Kgs. 25:29–30).

This is an image so out of character with its context that it calls for discussion. We had just witnessed in the narrative about Zedekiah, the last of the Judean kings, how his sons were slaughtered in the king's presence, and then the king was blinded before being bound and taken off to Babylon as a prisoner. Jerusalem and the temple had been torn down and burned. Tracking voice through these chapters reveals that even the mode of presentation had withdrawn into a passive stance, simply describing the devastation of the region. A deathly silence overshadows the story. There are no speeches, with but one exception. Gedaliah, son of Ahikam, son of Saphan—these are names familiar from the better days under Josiah—was appointed governor by Nebuchadnezzar over those left behind in Judah. Gedaliah said, "Do not be afraid of the servants of the Chaldeans. Stay in the land, and serve the king of Babylon, and it will go well with you" (2 Kgs. 25:24).

This too is a speech quite unexpected—that is, unless one hears the echoes of previous stories in the collection that also comes from the wilderness experience: of Elijah finding water in the Wadi Cherith; of ravens nourishing him with bread and meat; of oil that did not fail the widow-woman and her son in a time of famine. Yes, Abiathar was silenced by Solomon, and Ahijah of Shiloh was betrayed by Jeroboam I, and Ahab did take Naboth's vineyard. But there was also Obadiah over the house of Ahab, and the priest Jehoiada, protector of Jehoash of Judah. Images of liberation and freedom emerge from wilderness settings again and again. One is reminded of YHWH's holy mountain, flaming in the wilderness, calling Israel into being (Deut. 5).

Now, Jehoiachin is presented to us in relationship with a Babylonian king, a relationship one would not expect, unless Gedaliah, himself rooted in Mushite Levite tradition, was reminding us of the Mosaic vision: "Don't be afraid...stay in the land, serve the king of Babylon...and it will go well with you" (2 Kgs. 25:34). God is not limited to the boundaries of Judah.

The destructive power of the wilderness is unrelenting, however. We learn of a group from the royal family who assassinated Gedaliah, probably viewing Gedaliah's political views as treasonous. We read of a remnant fleeing to Egypt. From Egypt to Egypt as one scholar has put it,[4] from dust to dust; this seems to be the human condition, but there is also a resiliency to this spiritual pathway of the Mushite Levite family. Its foundation is that YHWH understands the wilderness experience and, from its substance, can bring forth new creation. These are moments of glory. The image of Jehoiachin eating as an honored guest with a king of Babylon affirms anew that YHWH can use even desolate places to provide "a portion day by day all the days of [our] lives" (2 Kgs. 25:30).

The Mushite Levite Vision

It is our claim that when compared with the Zadokite vision, the Mushite Levite priestly family: (1) humanized the narrative, (2) named the powers, and (3) defined the holy in terms of healing. All of these would be values held by those who live on the margins. As a result, the presentation of David and Solomon in Samuel/Kings is different from that encountered in Chronicles. Not only is the reader permitted to see David as he grew old and frail, but even in his prime we see a leader with mixed attributes.

David

David was a survivor. He was one who could help demystify the wilderness. He was a man of action. He was good at what he did. He brought engaging the dangers of the desolate places within the range of the possible. One of the powers of the wilderness is its capacity to induce fear and panic, thereby paralyzing those lost in its grip. David could keep one step ahead of the demons. David was not divine or perfect; thus, he was the kind of hero with whom one could identify. He gathered followers. David knew how to humanize the desert places.

David spent a number of years fleeing Saul, living as an outlaw. To survive he created his own rules in a dangerous world. He gathered around him other free spirits. He could even survive feigning madness among the alien Philistines. Those who lived on the margins would admire such a person. In a sense, he was his own man.

Occasionally he crossed over the line, as in the incident of getting Bathsheba pregnant and then trying to cover it up by arranging to

---

[4]The phrase "from Egypt to Egypt" is borrowed from Friedman, ibid.

have her husband, Uriah, killed in battle. Nathan made it very clear that that kind of abuse of power was wrong.

We know that not everyone liked David. There were enough discontented people in the kingdom of David that Absalom could lead a rebellion against his father, a rebellion powerful enough to force David to leave Jerusalem. And there were those like Shemei who were angry enough with David to curse him as he left.

Yet Abiathar found in David a kindred spirit, one to whom he could turn when he was desperate after the massacre of the priests at Nob. David could make a mistake, acknowledge it, and move on. He was the kind of person who could build a nation because he knew how to create relationships and let God be God. The latter would suggest that for the Deuteronomist, as central as David was for the narrative, he was not the primary norm from which the reading of the monarchy was being made. It appears that Moses and the commandments voiced by God at the flaming mountain in the wilderness were the platform from which the story was being told. David was at home in the wilderness, and when he showed compassion for the vulnerable, he was at his best. When he abused power, the narrator was quite prepared to criticize his actions.

Solomon

Solomon took the monarchy too far. Certainly this is evident in his old age: "Solomon was building a high place for Chemosh, the filth of Moab, on the mountain which is east of Jerusalem, and for Molech, the filth of the Ammonites" (1 Kgs. 11:7). This, of course, was in direct violation of the first commandment and became grounds for YHWH's decision, "I will surely tear the kingdom from you" (1 Kgs. 11:11).

Solomon's primary builder was Hiram from Tyre. It is interesting that the Deuteronomist should mention that Hiram's mother was a widowed woman (1 Kgs. 7:14) from the tribe of Naphtali. Even here on the threshold of a description of Solomon's great accomplishment in building God's house, it is strange that the introduction of Hiram should include a reference to his mother as a widow. It is a bit unsettling too that on the completion of Hiram's work, Solomon gave Hiram twenty cities in Galilee. "Hiram went out from Tyre to see the cities that Solomon had given him, but they were not satisfactory in his eyes" (1 Kgs. 9:12).

When such details are added to the narrative about Solomon, the earlier discussion of the speeches by both David and Solomon in private places, plus the dismissal of Abiathar, one begins to wonder about the description of the building of God's house itself. It was certainly a spectacular accomplishment, but does its very elaborateness conceal another message from the author? As with Saul and Absalom and Eliab, people look at externals; God looks on the inside.

Special mention was made of moving the ark of YHWH and the tent of meeting into the holy of holies (1 Kgs. 8:4) to reside in the space under the wings of the cherubim. In the ark were "the two tablets of stone which Moses put to rest there at Horeb when YHWH made a covenant with the Israelites, when they went out from the land of Egypt" (1 Kgs. 8:9). A Mushite Levite priest might read the occasion differently than a Zadokite priest. Just as the primary hero had shifted from Moses to Aaron in the Zadokite telling of some of the wilderness narratives, so now architecturally the central icon of the earlier period—the movable ark of the covenant and tent of meeting—were being transferred to the holy of holies in the temple. Primary jurisdiction was also being transferred to Aaronid priests.

One is reminded of Nathan's speech to David in 2 Samuel 7 quoting YHWH, "Thus says YHWH: Will you build me a house for me to reside [in]? Surely I have not resided in a house since the day I brought up the Israelites from Egypt even to this day; rather I have been moving about in a tent and in a tabernacle…have I ever uttered a word with one of the tribal chiefs of Israel whom I commanded to shepherd my people Israel, saying: 'Why have you not built me a house of cedar?'" (2 Sam. 7:6–7).

The very detail and magnificence of the structure carries a double message. On the one hand, it was inspiring: "When the priests came out of the holy place, the cloud filled the house of YHWH, and the priests were not able to stand, to minister in front of the cloud, for the glory of YHWH filled the house of YHWH" (1 Kgs. 8:11).

On the other hand, we have a reminder from YHWH to Solomon in a later speech: "If you turn aside from me, you and your descendants, and do not keep my commandments and my statutes, which I have put before you, but you go and serve other gods and worship them, then I will cut off Israel from the face of the land, that I have given them; and the house which I have dedicated for my name I will cast out of my sight" (1 Kgs. 9:6–7).

As the summary of Solomon's building projects gets longer and longer and the lists of forced labor required to accomplish the tasks grow, even the visit from the Queen of Sheba begins to carry a double message. Solomon at the very height of his power begins to remind us of the overweight and blind Eli on the verge of falling off his stool, which begins to happen on that fateful day when Ahijah of Shiloh met Jeroboam—whose mother was also a widow woman (1 Kgs. 11:26)—outside Jerusalem on the way. "The two of them were alone in the open country" (1 Kgs. 11:20), and Ahijah tore his garment into twelve pieces.

4

A POLITICS OF CENTRALIZATION
David, Solomon, and the Levites

W e have focused our attention on a comparison of the narrative histories of Chronicles and Samuel/Kings. We have proposed that even though the content of these histories appears to be centered on the kings of Judah and Israel, the stories are told in such a way that one sees reflected in the narratives the values and worldviews of two priestly families of ancient Israel. Also proposed is that the catalyst for the different perceptions is rooted in the respective experiences of the priestly families with political power centered in the kings of the monarchy. Of particular significance was David's choice of two high priests and then Solomon's choice of one. While it oversimplifies things to construct a comparative chart, the following list does help to orient our thinking and summarize where we have been thus far.

Comparative Spiritual Pathways

Aaronid Zadokites	Mushite Levites
Center of Meaning: Jerusalem/Zion	Center of Meaning: Wilderness/Horeb
Sacred Space: Inside (temple)	Sacred Space: Outside (wilderness)
Theophany as fire in temple	Theophany as fire at Horeb
God consumes temple sacrifice	God speaks normative word
Believers withdraw into holy	Believers drawn into relationships
The holy embraces perfection	The holy embraces imperfection
The holy reaches toward discipline	The holy reaches toward wholeness
God establishes boundaries	God breaks through boundaries
From vulnerability to stability	From slavery to freedom
Genealogy: Zadok to Aaron	Genealogy: Abiathar to Moses

In earlier chapters, we have also proposed that the movement of our discussion is drawing its clues from archaeology. Like the excavator of a tell, we have begun at the top of a literary mound, which is the period of its latest date. As the search proceeds through the strata into the heart of the mound, one is working backward through time. Taking sacred story seriously as a means of communicating truth about one's experience of the holy, our goal has been to locate a center of meaning within the various strata, then from the perspective of that stance fill out the implications for understanding the spiritual life. Once we have reached bedrock, as it were, it becomes possible to reconstruct a history of the tell, reorganizing the data into an interpretive whole.

We have arrived at a point now where we seek to move to a literary stratum that is earlier than either the Chronicler or the Deuteronomist. This raises some issues concerning the documentary hypothesis and the usefulness of its proposals as a guide to earlier literary strata within the Hebrew Bible.[1] Our discussion will center on the Yahwist (J) and what we can learn about priests and priesthood within that literary stratum.

Since this is the third block of material we are investigating, a preliminary summary of our conclusions is in order. This third and earlier cluster of literary strata reflects the creation of the monarchy under David and Solomon. Here the center of meaning has shifted

---

[1]For a readable presentation of the documentary hypothesis and one that also recognizes the central role played by priestly families, see Richard Elliott Friedman, *Who Wrote the Bible?* 2d ed. (New York: Harper & Row, 1990).

from a social system that affirmed shared power grounded in local tribal sanctuaries to a centralized social system whose center was Jerusalem/Zion. Israel's first epic narrative was the Yahwist's (J) linkage of originally separate, local, tribal, sacred stories into the framework of a genealogical network, creating a kingdom conceived as sons of Jacob united in covenant before Yahweh.[2] Older traditions were recast into a centralized system offering myth and ritual support for the monarchy. While the Davidic construct included two high priests, Abiathar and Zadok, the Solomonic construct affirmed only Zadok, whose genealogical connection to the wilderness period was with Aaron. The Mosaic authority of the northern house of Eli was delegitimized. What we will see in both the realms of priestly families and local sanctuaries is the movement from many to one.

Levi

Historical criticism, with its frequent practice of identifying literary sources as an explanation for why there appear to be breaks and inconsistencies in a text, is often criticized for not paying sufficient attention to the final form of the received text. To balance this neglect, of late there has been considerable interest in applying insight from the world of literary criticism to an interpretation of the received text. For instance, Robert Polzin has shown that it is possible to interpret the texts of the Deuteronomistic history without resorting to source division.[3] Rather, he has demonstrated the usefulness of the literary critical theory of the Russian school founded by Mikhail Bakhtin, to show how the biblical text gives evidence of being intentionally and creatively multivoiced. As is evident in the previous chapters, we have been heavily influenced by this methodical approach to our reading of the text.

On the other hand, Richard Elliott Friedman has shown that there is still room for source criticism when dealing with large blocks of material.[4] He has argued that the history of biblical scholarship

---

[2]See the very helpful article by Frank Moore Cross, "Kinship and Covenant in Ancient Israel," in *From Epic to Canon: History and Literature in Ancient Israel* (Baltimore: Johns Hopkins University Press, 1998), 3–21.

[3]See Robert Polzin, *Moses and the Deuteronomist* (San Francisco: Harper & Row, 1980); *Samuel and the Deuteronomist* (San Francisco: Harper & Row, 1989); and *David and the Deuteronomist* (Bloomington, Ind.: Indiana University Press, 1993).

[4]Richard Elliott Friedman, *The Hidden Book in the Bible* (San Francisco: Harper San Francisco, 1998), 3–32.

has reached a point where we can now pull together some of the commonalities that have been isolated into sources and documents over the last couple of centuries. One such example is the Yahwist. He recently began an investigation of the similarities between the Yahwist Document (J) and the Court History of David. He has proposed—even surprising himself—that they belong to the same literary work; indeed, he suggests the work is the first extended prose narrative history there is.[5]

Friedman's proposal is of interest to us because he proposes that the conclusion of the full Yahwistic history ends with the same first two chapters of 1 Kings we looked at earlier as part of the Deuteronomistic history. This would mean that the Deuteronomist has used the Yahwist (J) as one of his written sources. Since this Yahwistic document does mention Levi and Levites, it is important that we investigate the matter further.

One of the literary critical insights we have been pursuing in our reading of biblical texts is the possibility that a single integrated text can carry multiple voices. That same approach works well here without denying the usefulness of recognizing the author's use of an established written source. For instance, we have noted there can sometimes be a concealed message from the author to the reader that is different from, and may even contradict, the surface message of the text. This became identifiable by the way the narrator led the reader into narrative spaces that provided an alternate perspective on an event or speech.

So here, the Deuteronomist could alter the reading of an utterance rooted in a Yahwistic text without distorting the written text. Within the Yahwistic context, the surface text of 1 Kings 1—2 could carry the primary meaning for the Yahwist's audience. If the Deuteronomist included 1 Kings 1—2 as material from a source, a different reading of the text could result if approached from the larger context of the Deuteronomistic history. The ultimate semantic authority of the Deuteronomist's reading could be different from that of the Yahwist. When we looked at 1 Kings 1—2 above, we did so from the Deuteronomist's perspective. We propose now to look back into the Yahwistic history to those passages that deal with Levi and Levites. We will ask, Does the Yahwistic history read the place of Levi and the Levites in the scheme of things differently? We will conclude that yes,

---

[5]Ibid., 3.

the Yahwist views Levi and the Levites as being outside any priestly circle. The Yahwist's agenda is focused more on the secular goal of legitimizing the move toward monarchy. Religious institutions will have to rethink their places in the larger social order along with everyone else.

Of particular interest to us is Friedman's observation that in the Court History of David, there is the narrative about four sons of David: Amnon, Absalom, Adonijah, and Solomon.[6] As we have seen, it was the fourth son of David, Solomon, who successfully rose to power and succeeded David as king. In the narrative about Jacob, there were also presented the first four sons of Jacob from Leah: Reuben, Simeon, Levi, and Judah. Not only is it of interest that Levi is in the list, but once again it was the fourth son of Jacob who rose to prominence as the ancestor of the tribe of Judah. David was from the tribe of Judah. It has long been recognized that the Yahwistic history reflects the worldview and values of Judah, that is, the south. We have argued thus far, and most agree, that the Deuteronomistic history reflects the northern values of Israel; thus, there is reason to expect that the Yahwist's presentation of Levi and Levites would be different from that encountered in the Deuteronomist's work.

Simeon and Levi (Gen. 34)

The story of the rape of Dinah, daughter of Jacob and Leah, shows some remarkable parallels to the story of the rape of Tamar in the Court History of David. This was one of the lines of evidence that has led Friedman to argue that these stories come from a much larger, single work, written by the same author.[7] The narrator brings the reader into the social space of family life. It is in this space of family, rather than in any religious social space, that we meet Levi. We encounter the dynamics of the honor/shame system.[8] This system assumes that the honor of the head of household is embedded in the honor of all those who come under his jurisdiction in what we would call an extended family. Daughters were expected to be shame-ful, which was a good quality. It meant that the daughter had internalized

---

[6]Ibid., 8.

[7]Ibid.

[8]See the excellent discussion of the honor/shame system in Bruce J. Malina, "Honor and Shame: Pivotal Values of the First-Century Mediterranean World," *The New Testament World: Insights from Cultural Anthropology,* 2d ed. (Louisville, Ky.: Westminster/John Knox Press, 1993), 28–62.

the social boundaries of appropriate behavior. To be shame-less would make her dangerous in that her behavior would be unpredictable, thereby exposing the honor of the head of household to threat.

Should a woman be raped by someone outside the family, the offense was not only against the woman but extended to the head of household as well. To defile someone under his jurisdiction defiled his honor. This challenge to his honor called for response. It was incumbent particularly on brothers to avenge such an act against a sister. Bruce Malina has shown that in what was largely an arranged marriage between families, the strongest emotional ties often existed between brothers and sisters.[9] To avenge such an act against a sister would also serve the function of restoring the father's sense of honor.

Dinah was a daughter of Leah, which linked her particularly to the four sons of Leah—Reuben, Simeon, Levi, and Judah—her brothers. Her father was Jacob, the head of household. Dinah "went out to visit the women of the region" (Gen. 34:1). That would be acceptable because, even if unaccompanied by a male, her intent was to remain in women's space. Shechem, son of Hamor, a Hivite, saw her and had sex with her. This act, of course, dishonored both her and Jacob. The narrator tells us Shechem loved the girl and asked his father Hamor to arrange for a wedding: "Get me this girl to be my wife" (Gen. 34:4). This would require the negotiation of a bridal price between the two heads of household in order for this to be an honorable exchange. The negotiation was off to a bad start, however, as Jacob entered the exchange dishonored.

When Jacob heard that Shechem had defiled his daughter, his sons were with the cattle in the field, so he kept quiet until they returned. Hamor approached Jacob. When Jacob's sons heard what had happened, "they were indignant and very angry, because he had committed an outrage in Israel by lying with Jacob's daughter, for such a thing ought not to be done" (Gen. 34:7).

Hamor opened the negotiations by offering an opportunity for intermarriage among their two peoples. Not only could marriage happen between Shechem and Dinah but, "give your daughters to us, and take our daughters for yourselves. You shall live with us; and the land shall be open to you; live and trade in it, and get property in it" (Gen. 34:10). Shechem, too, anxious to marry Dinah, offered to pay whatever the father and sons requested for a bridal price.

---

[9] Ibid., 122.

The narrator reveals to the reader that Jacob's sons were still angry at being dishonored, which would be grounds for their negotiating deceptively. "The sons of Jacob answered Shechem and his father Hamor deceitfully, because he had defiled their sister Dinah" (Gen. 34:13). The Hivites were uncircumcised, which would make it unlawful for them to enter into marriage negotiations. But if they would agree to be circumcised, "then we will give our daughters to you, and we will take your daughters for ourselves, and we will live among you and become one people" (Gen. 34:14).

Hamor and Shechem agreed to the terms and convinced their people to do the same. The land was big enough for the two peoples to live together. Besides, "Will not their livestock, their property, and all their animals be ours?" Shechem said to his people (Gen. 34:23). All the males were circumcised, and on the third day, when they were still in a weakened condition, they were attacked by two of Jacob's sons, Simeon and Levi. Simeon and Levi killed every male, rescued Dinah from Shechem's house, and plundered the city "because their sister had been defiled" (Gen. 34:27).

Jacob's public response to Simeon and Levi was harsh. "You have brought trouble on me by making me odious to the habitants of the land, the Canaanites and the Perizzites; my numbers are few, and if they gather themselves against me and attack me, I shall be destroyed" (Gen. 34:31). With this response, the narrator has revealed to the reader the complexity of being head of household charged with upholding the honor of the family name. Two challenges to Jacob came together, both demanding responses. Jacob had to reprimand his sons, Simeon and Levi, publicly because the negotiations with Hamor's family had been violated. But privately, Simeon and Levi had avenged the dishonor brought to the family by Shechem's rape of Dinah. In Jacob's blessing of his sons at his death, there are these words for Simeon and Levi:

Weapons of violence are their swords.
May I never come into their council;
may I not be joined to their company—
for in their anger they killed men,
and at their whim they hamstrung oxen.
Cursed be their anger, for it is fierce,
and their wrath, for it is cruel.
I will divide them in Jacob,
and scatter them in Israel. (Gen. 49:5–7)

For our purposes, there is nothing in this earlier story in Genesis about Levi that gives us a hint that here is a tribe destined for religious leadership; indeed, quite the opposite: "I will divide them in Jacob, and scatter them in Israel" (Gen. 49:7). The fall of the house of Eli and the dismissal of Abiathar during the reign of Solomon would be consistent with the tone of this earlier story. A more reliable priesthood was sought.

Micah and the Levite (Judg. 17)

Friedman suggests that the implied author of the Yahwistic material was "from a class that was educated and had access to writing materials...The author was probably a layperson, not a priest. The work is different from the biblical works that are ascribed to authors who were priests."[10] We would agree on this point; whereas both Chronicles and the Deuteronomistic history seem to structure the narrative from within the special interests of a priestly family, though each tradition highlights a different priestly family, the Yahwist's comments on Levi and the Levites fit easily into observations made by someone outside any group with specific priestly concerns.

Two stories about a Levite at the end of Judges attributed to the Yahwist further illustrate this point. The first is a story about a man from Ephraim named Micah. Some money, exchanged between him and his mother, was used to make "an idol of cast metal" (Judg. 17:4) to be placed at a shrine located in Micah's home. In addition Micah "made an ephod and teraphim, and installed one of his sons, who became his priest" (Judg. 17:5). Then follows a refrain that repeats a number of times: "In those days there was no king in Israel. All people did what was right in their own eyes" (Judg. 17:6). Given the whole Yahwistic work ending as proposed, with the establishment of the kingdom under David and Solomon and the eventual centralization of religious practice, Micah's designation of one of his sons as priest over a household sanctuary, while probably a prevalent practice, was less than ideal when viewed from the eyes of the Yahwist.

The narrative then proceeds to tell of a Levite from Bethlehem, David's birthplace, looking for a place to live in the mountains of Ephraim. Micah asked him, "Where are you coming from?" and he answered, "I am a Levite of Bethlehem in Judah, and I am going to

---

[10]Friedman, *The Hidden Book in the Bible*, 51.

live wherever I can find a place" (Judg. 17:9). Micah said, "Stay with me, and be to me a father and a priest, and I will give you ten pieces of silver a year, a set of clothes, and your living" (Judg. 17:10). The Levite came.

This is a picture consistent with Genesis 49, of Levites scattered among the tribes looking for whatever place they can to make a living. Apparently they can hire themselves out as priests; and to have a Levite as priest was desirable. Micah said, "Now I know that the Lord will prosper me, because the Levite has become my priest" (Judg. 17:13). Then the refrain: In those days there was no king in Israel.

Dan and Micah's Levite (Judg. 18)

Then the story continues with reference to the tribe of Dan, also looking for a place to settle. "The tribe of the Danites was seeking for itself a territory to live in; for until then no territory among the tribes of Israel had been allotted to them" (Judg. 18:1). They sent out five warriors in advance to spy out the land, and "when they came to the hill country of Ephraim, to the house of Micah, they stayed there" (Judg. 18:2). They recognized the Bethlehemite accent of the Levite and asked him who he was and what brought him to Ephraim. The Levite told them about how Micah had hired him on as his priest.

Since one of the functions of a priest was to predict the success of proposed plans, they inquired of him whether or not their seeking a place to settle would be successful. The Levite responded, "Go in peace. The mission you are on is under the eye of the Lord" (Judg. 18:6). They discovered that the land before them was wide open, desirable, and far from the threat of the Sidonians. They reported to the tribe that they should go forward and possess the land.

On their way to Ephraim, this time with the six hundred warriors from Dan, they stopped again at Micah's house. "They took the idol of cast metal, the ephod, and the teraphim. The priest said to them, 'What are you doing?' They said to him, 'Keep quiet! Put your hand over your mouth, and come with us, and be to us a father and a priest. Is it better for you to be priest to the house of one person, or to be priest to a tribe and clan in Israel?' Then the priest accepted the offer. He took the ephod, the teraphim, and the idol, and went along with the people" (Judg. 18:18–21).

This narrative was probably played out again and again as the political process of centralization unfolded under the leadership of

David and Solomon. People were being asked to give up their local and tribal allegiances for the larger "family of Israel." Micah pursued them, but to no avail. "When Micah saw that they were too strong for him, he turned and went back to his home" (Judg. 18:26). "Then the Danites set up the idol for themselves. Jonathan son of Gershom, son of Moses,[11] and his sons were priests to the tribe of the Danites until the time the land went into captivity. So they maintained as their own Micah's idol that he had made, as long as the house of God was at Shiloh" (Judg. 18:30–31).

This story would suggest that prior to centralization of the religious establishment at Jerusalem, in the north Shiloh was a very important, though one of many, sanctuary at which one could worship YHWH. At Dan the sanctuary appears to be in the hands of the Mushite Levites, given the genealogy of Jonathan, Gershom, Moses. To give ritual expression to the centralization process, it would eventually become necessary to move the ark of the covenant and the tent of meeting to Jerusalem. Like Micah, there may have been some not fully enthusiastic about the shift.

The Levite and His Concubine (Judg. 19)

Another story about a Levite is found in the closing chapters of Judges. We discussed earlier the Deuteronomistic narrative about the time when Ahijah of Shiloh approached Jeroboam to announce to him that YHWH was about to tear the kingdom from Solomon; he reinforced the message with the symbolic gesture of tearing Jeroboam's robe into twelve pieces. He gave Jeroboam ten torn pieces, saying, "Behold, I am tearing the kingdom from the hand of Solomon, and I will give you ten tribes" (1 Kgs. 11:30–31).

Admittedly, that image is from a later section in the Deuteronomistic history, but the gesture of tearing into pieces or cutting something into twelve parts may have had a longer history in the premonarchic period. It seems to be a mechanism used by charismatic leaders during the period of the judges to muster troops for battle. Since there was no king in the land who could simply order a standing, professional army to action, some means of persuasion had to be used.

In one of the early pictures of Saul, we see him plowing in a field behind his oxen. He received word from Jabesh-gilead that they were

---

[11]Following the Greek.

under attack from Nahash the Ammonite, who threatened to "gouge out everyone's right eye, and thus put disgrace upon all Israel" (1 Sam. 11:2). The spirit of God filled Saul with anger; when he heard it, "he took a yoke of oxen, and cut them in pieces and sent them throughout all the territory of Israel by messengers, saying, 'Whoever does not come out after Saul and Samuel, so shall it be done to his oxen!' Then the dread of the Lord fell upon the people, and they came out as one. When he mustered them at Bezek, those from Israel were three hundred thousand, and those from Judah seventy thousand" (1 Sam. 11:7–8).

In the Song of Deborah, Judges 5, we learn that not everyone always responded to a call to arms. In effect, Israel had to depend on a volunteer, even ad hoc, army. This had the advantage of not concentrating too much power in a central person or place; but it was not an efficient way to deal with military crises.

With this in mind, we turn to another story about a Levite, "in the days when there was no king in Israel." There was a Levite living in the hills of Ephraim who took himself a concubine woman from Bethlehem. "But his concubine became angry with him, and she went away from him to her father's house at Bethlehem in Judah, and was there some four months" (Judg. 19:2). The Levite went to Bethlehem to retrieve his concubine and return to Ephraim. On their way home, nightfall approached, and they sought shelter in Gibeah, which was in Benjamin. They were planning to spend the night in the square, but instead were invited by an old man to spend the night at his house.

"While they were enjoying themselves, the men of the city, a perverse lot, surrounded the house, and started pounding on the door. They said to the old man, the master of the house, 'Bring out the man who came into your house so that we may have intercourse with him'"(Judg. 19:22). Since within a tribal system of ethics it is honorable to protect an invited guest from danger, the old man responded, "Here are my virgin daughter and his concubine; let me bring them out now. Ravish them and do whatever you want to them; but against this man do not do such a vile thing" (Judg. 19:24).

The Levite's concubine was abused by the crowd all night until morning, at which time she was left, "lying at the door of the house, with her hands on the threshold" (Judg. 19:27). Next day the Levite said, "Get up, we are going," but there was no answer. He set out for his home. "When he had entered his house, he took a knife, and grasping his concubine he cut her into twelve pieces, limb by limb, and sent her throughout all the territory of Israel" (Judg. 19:29); whereupon the tribes of Israel took counsel and a battle against Benjamin and Gibeah ensued. Eventually Israel won, but it raised the theological problem of whether or not Israel should be fighting against one of its own, perhaps even to the point of extinguishing one of the tribes. Within the social organization of tribes, intertribal warfare is not unusual; but here the question is being raised, Is it time to move beyond that system, with its practices, to a different kind of social and political organization?

The prospect of disorder reaching such a point where household guests were threatened by gang rape, paralleled in the Lot at Sodom and Gomorrah story, plus the extended abuse of the Levite's concubine and subsequent cutting her up in pieces, a familiar practice to muster troops for battle—without even assuring the reader that she was dead—would have been just as horrifying a story to the ancient hearer as it is to us. The message from the Yahwist appears to be: Human nature being what it is, it is time for the more civilized order and political system of a monarchy. We need a king in the land.

Once again, there is nothing about the Levite that tells us he is a religious figure. But there are working sanctuaries in the narrative, places where people may go for predictions about the outcomes of events. The sanctuary of Bethel appears to be in charge of Aaronids, given the genealogy Phinehas, Eleazar, and Aaron (Judg. 20:28). This Phinehas would be a different Phinehas from the one we met in the Samuel–Eli story. Recall also that the sanctuary at Dan appeared to be in Mushite Levite hands: Jonathan, Gershom, Moses (Judg. 18:30).

"Then the eyes of both were opened" (Gen. 3:7)

The Yahwist was speaking from outside priestly circles and thus stands outside our interest in the world of the priests; but the Yahwist did speak about Levi and Levites and did include in the narrative observations about sanctuaries and priestly practice. The perspective brought by the Yahwist for our discussion is a view from the outside. The driving energy and worldview of the Yahwist would impact the structure of the early religious system, so it is worth our while to say a few words about the agenda of the Yahwist.

One of the roles of a creation story is to establish a paradigm within which to understand the logic of behavior and events. The garden of Eden story in Genesis 2—3 begins the Yahwist's narrative and does establish such a paradigm. Thorkild Jacobsen once observed that the Gilgamesh epic was a "story about growing up."[12] In narrative form, the storyteller was making observations about the process of growing up, both individually and communally. In our culture we have the benefit of our language and study of the social sciences to address such issues.

The Yahwist in the garden of Eden story, I would argue, is offering ancient Israel and us another such story about growing up. This was the challenge and agenda facing the Yahwist. The move toward monarchy would entail fundamental changes in the internal structures of the social order and in the way individuals viewed the world. It would be both exhilarating and frightening. To let go of the old and embrace the new would involve risks, some predictable and some unforeseen.

The garden of Eden story begins with an image of the lifeless state, envisioned as the boundless expanse of desert. This latter, of course, was a readily available sight in the Middle East. "For the Lord God had not caused it to rain upon the earth, and there was no one to till the ground" (Gen. 2:5). In such a setting, a metaphor for the emergence of life would naturally be understood in the language of an oasis in the desert. The garden contains all the prerequisites to sustain life: water, shade, food, leaves for clothing. In this garden were two special trees: the tree of life and the tree of the knowledge of good and bad.

If we allow that the man and woman stand for all men and women, the narrative becomes a description of how each of us comes to be human, how our humanity is created. Initially, we are born into innocence. When we come to consciousness we find all our basic needs for survival provided for under the care of a protector. There are rules, usually not explained, since we are still too young to understand. We are expected to "just do it."

Then one day—in our culture, we would probably label the stage as adolescence—the humans begin to ask questions: "Why? Why not?"

---

[12]Thorkild Jacobsen, *The Treasures of Darkness: A History of Mesopotamian Religion* (New Haven, Conn.: Yale University Press, 1976), 219.

This is an extremely important moment in our growing up, but not without risks. "So when the woman saw that the tree was good for food, and that it was a delight to the eyes, and that the tree was to be desired to make one wise, she took of its fruit and gave some to her husband, who was with her, and he ate. Then the eyes of both were opened, and they knew that they were naked" (Gen. 2:6–7).

On that day, when we make a decision on our own, without checking in with the authority figure over our lives, the way we see the world changes forever. Yes, there is a "fall," in the sense that we fall from innocence. The invisible shield that has protected us from the harshness of life falls away, and the world is much bigger and more dangerous than we previously knew. Our eyes are opened, and we are aware of our nakedness.

We have also, however, taken one step toward maturity, an awakening, as it were. "The eyes of both were opened." I say one step because the narrative also acknowledges that initially, as adolescents, we often do not bear responsibility for our choices. The man blamed the woman; the woman blamed the serpent. God, as authority figure, used the opportunity to teach us that we must bear responsibility for our actions and choices. Thus, God introduced the consequences. Outside the garden of innocence the humans begin their long journey toward maturity, seeking to re-relate with God, this time by free choice and not as initially in innocence.

This process of growing up operates socially as well as individually. Groups can also mature and grow up. The Yahwist was constructing a pathway that would move people from the more limited lifestyle of tribal interaction to the larger, more inclusive social order of the monarchy. This would be accomplished under David and Solomon. People would lose the familiarity of individual tribal patterns; but at the same time, if they could embrace the changes, they would join the family of nations in the larger, ancient Near East. It would be an experience both exhilarating and frightening.

One of the components of the shift impacting the religious system would be the requirement to close down the local sanctuaries, with all their tribal history and allegiances, and open up a new, single center for the monarchy where YHWH would reside. This would be Jerusalem. The promise and contribution made by the Yahwist as writer was that individual tribal groups would not lose their sacred stories. Stories that gave expression to their voice would be woven into a narrative that would become Israel's first epic, conceived as a family story composed of sons of Jacob united in covenant before YHWH. This epic would affirm connections among groups that originally may have lived quite independently from one another. This family would be called Israel.

From Abraham to Solomon

One of the local collections of narratives clustering around the tribal ancestor Abraham, associated initially with the sanctuary at Hebron, was incorporated into the larger epic marking the introduction of the theme of promise and fulfillment. In a speech from YHWH to Abraham, a central theme of Israel's becoming a great kingdom finds expression: "Go from your country and your kindred and your father's house to the land that I will show you. I will make of you a great nation, and I will bless you, and make your name great, so that you will be a blessing. I will bless those who bless you, and the one who curses you I will curse; and in you all the families of the earth shall be blessed" (Gen. 12:2–3). It is within this larger frame of promise and fulfillment that the gathering of local stories was cast.

The theme was traced through the narratives about Isaac, Jacob/ Israel, and his twelve sons [tribes]. In an oracle of Balaam, we read, "A star shall come out of Jacob, and a scepter shall rise out of Israel" (Num. 24:17). If Friedman is correct, the Yahwist's epic extends through the narratives about David and Solomon in what we now know as 1 Kings 1—2. The Yahwist's vision achieved its fulfillment with Solomon's consolidation of his power: "So the kingdom was established in the hand of Solomon" (1 Kgs. 2:46).

In the Yahwist's account, the surface message to J's implied audience was to praise David and Solomon for their achievement. The curse of the Mushite Levite house of Eli and his incompetent sons, Hophni and Phinehas, gave credence to Solomon's firing of Abiathar and elevation of Zadok to sole high priest, a priest who could be trusted.

As we noted above, the Deuteronomist could take that same text and, by moving the reader to alternate narrative spaces, shift the perspective to the event of Abiathar's dismissal. The reader is led to conclude by the Deuteronomist's rendering that Solomon's act was motivated more by political opportunism than service to Yahweh. A concealed message suggesting Solomon's arrogance begins to emerge and culminates in the meeting between Ahijah of Shiloh and Jeroboam, ultimately resulting in civil war. In the hands of the Deuteronomist we witness reversal; what began as praise, ends with a curse.

The Elohist (North) and Priestly (South) Documents
Exodus 32 (Elohist)

In contrast to what we have called the secular orientation of the Yahwist, the Elohist and Priestly documents are much more priestly oriented than J. Materials associated with the north, such as the E and D documents, are much more open to affirming Levites in a priestly role and Moses as the ancestor to priestly leadership.

Exodus 32 is a case in point. This is an E story, from the north, about Aaron and the golden calf. Moses was clearly in charge and gives no evidence of a speech problem. Moses had ascended the mountain at Sinai and apparently stayed away longer than the people had anticipated. "The people gathered around Aaron, and said to him, 'Come, make gods for us, who shall go before us; as for this Moses, the man who brought us up out of the land of Egypt, we do not know what has become of him'" (Exod. 32:1).

Aaron acceded to their request, gathered up their jewelry, cast it into a mold, and made it into a molten calf. When Aaron saw this, he built an altar before it, and Aaron announced, "Tomorrow shall be a festival to the Lord" (Exod. 32:5).

Of course YHWH was angry, but Moses interceded for the people. On his way down from the mountain Joshua heard the sound of the people and said to Moses, "There is a noise of war in the camp" (Exod. 32:17). Moses said no, it was the sound of song. They arrived near the camp and saw the calf and the dancing of the people. Moses grew very angry, smashed the tablets he was carrying, ground the calf into powder, strewed it upon the water, and made the Israelites drink it.

Then Moses confronted Aaron. Aaron explained what had happened: "Moses saw that the people were running wild (for Aaron had let them run wild, to the derision of their enemies)" (Exod. 32:25). This seems to be a pretty clear message from the author to the reader that Aaron did not have what it takes to lead the people. As soon as Moses is removed from the scene, the people lose direction and break the commandments prohibiting the worship of other gods and the creation of molten images. Scholars have often made the connection between this story and the creation of golden calves at Bethel and

Dan by Jeroboam I.[13] We noted in our discussion of Jeroboam that Ahijah of Shiloh was particularly concerned that Mushite Levites were not being hired as priests at Jeroboam's reopened sanctuaries.

We have illustrated how central the role of keeper of the sacred stories was in the telling of a narrative about Aaron displacing Moses as the primary spokesperson for YHWH in Exodus 4. We suggested this was a means to legitimize Solomon's choice of Zadok over the temple, after he had dismissed Abiathar. Here we have a Levite response. The counterclaim from those in Ahijah of Shiloh's camp was that only [Mushite] Levites were legitimate priests capable of leading the people.

To continue the Exodus 32 story, Moses announced at the gate of the camp, "Who is on the Lord's side? Come to me!" (Exod. 32:26). The narrator said, "All the sons of Levi gathered around him. He said to them, 'Thus says the Lord, the God of Israel, "Put your sword on your side, each of you! Go back and forth from gate to gate throughout the camp, and each of you kill your brother, your friend, and your neighbor."' The sons of Levi did as Moses commanded, and about three thousand of the people fell on that day. Moses said, 'Today you have ordained yourselves for the service of the Lord, each one at the cost of a son or a brother, and so you have brought a blessing on yourselves this day'" (Exod. 32:26–29).

In the J narrative of southern tradition, we have seen that Levi was capable of violent action, as against the Shechemites. In the blessing of Jacob, they are "scattered in Israel" (Gen. 49:7). Here in the Elohist's account, that violent energy is marshaled to serve the cause of YHWH's warranting a blessing, a blessing associated with ordination to the priestly office.

Leviticus 8—9 (The Priestly Document)

In contrast to the negative assessment of Aaron in Exodus 32, the Priestly document (P), which includes the book of Leviticus, affirms the leadership of Aaron in religious affairs. In chapter 8 and following, Moses is presented as officiating over an ordination ceremony that officially transfers the authority of the priesthood to the sons of Aaron. "The Lord spoke to Moses, saying, 'Take Aaron and his sons with him, the vestments, the anointing oil, the bull of sin offering, the two

---

[13]See the discussion of Exodus 32 in Friedman, *Who Wrote the Bible?* chap. 3.

rams, and the basket of unleavened bread; and assemble the whole congregation at the entrance of the tent of meeting.' And Moses did as the Lord commanded him...Moses said to the congregation, 'This is what the Lord has commanded to be done'" (Lev. 8:1–5). Within a series of sacrificial offerings, Aaron and his sons were consecrated to the priesthood. "Moses said, 'This is the thing that the Lord commanded you to do, so that the glory of the Lord may appear to you...Draw near to the altar'" (Lev. 9:6–7).

The date of the Priestly document has been debated. It would make sense for an early edition of the Priestly code to be in place during the reign of Hezekiah, who was ruling in Judah at the time of the fall of Israel. At such a time, there was probably an influx of northerners fleeing south before the threat of Assyria. We have seen that Hezekiah was a highly regarded king among both Zadokites and Mushite Levites. He received positive mention in both Kings and Chronicles, though for different reasons. It would be a logical time to reaffirm the Aaronid Zadokite control of the internal affairs of the temple. The Mushite Levite priests would be welcomed to the south as long as they recognized Aaronid Zadokites as the priests of the first order. In return, the northerners were promised that their sacred stories would not be lost. A second edition of the Israelite epic (JEP) would be dated to this time. It would be composed of the Yahwist's material plus the Priestly materials, augmented by some of the anti-Aaron material, like Exodus 32 and Numbers 12, from the north.[14]

Korah (Num. 16)

The ascendancy of the Aaronids seems to have absorbed other Levitical families such as the Korahites. The central issue in Numbers 16 is once again, Who shall speak for YHWH? "Moses said to Korah, 'Hear now, you Levites! Is it too little for you that the God of Israel has separated you from the congregation of Israel, to allow you to approach him in order to perform the duties of the Lord's tabernacle, and to stand before the congregation and serve them? He has allowed you to approach him and all your brother Levites with you; yet you seek the priesthood as well? Therefore you and all your company have gathered together against the Lord. What is Aaron that you rail against

---

[14]See the discussion of the Priestly material during the reign of Hezekiah in ibid., chaps. 11–12.

him?'" (Num. 16:8–11). A test was set up before YHWH. Moses and Aaron were confirmed; and Korah's followers were destroyed.

The catalyst for sorting through which groups were to emerge in the leadership position at the temple appears first to be David's choice of two high priests: Abiathar and Zadok, and Solomon's subsequent choice of Zadok. With royal power behind a group, other groups eventually fell away. That the Mushite Levites persisted after their dismissal by Solomon is a tribute to the authority in tradition of Moses and David.

Summary

This third, and earlier, cluster of literary strata reflects the creation of the monarchy under David and Solomon. Here the center of meaning has shifted from a social system that affirmed shared power grounded in local tribal sanctuaries to a centralized social system whose center was Jerusalem/Zion. David initiated some key moves to enable this transition. As many have noted, he moved the capital from Hebron to Jerusalem, a neutral and geographically central site with no previous Yahwistic connections; he formed a professional army, rather than rely totally upon tribal volunteers; he appointed two high priests to lead the religious establishment from Jerusalem, one reflecting northern views, the other southern views. Here we are suggesting that David hired an editor to collect and organize the sacred stories of the various tribal groups into a national epic.

Israel's first epic narrative was the Yahwist's (J) linkage of originally separate, local, tribal, sacred stories into the framework of a genealogical network, creating a kingdom conceived as sons of Jacob united in covenant before Yahweh. Older traditions were recast into a centralized system offering myth and ritual support for the monarchy. While the Davidic construct included two high priests, Abiathar and Zadok, the Solomonic construct affirmed only Zadok, whose genealogical connection to the wilderness period was with Aaron. The Mosaic authority of the northern house of Eli was delegitimized. What we see in both the realms of priestly families and local sanctuaries is the movement from many to one.

5

A POLITICS OF APOCALYPTIC
Beginning and End and
New Beginning

We have discovered that shifts in narrative space and narrative time are useful literary tools to alter perspective. It is precisely this possibility for movement that reenergizes voice when it is trapped within one plane of perception. The narrator can bring the reader or hearer to what looks like a dead end and then, with a reported speech or shift in perspective, move the entire setting to a new space or different time. Modern-day counselors may call such movement reframing. An old problem can be seen in a new light, and what were hidden options emerge as new possibilities.

Apocalyptic is a genre of perception that takes full advantage of this narrative strategy. Particularly with apocalyptic, our thesis about what the Bible is, bears repeating. We are assuming that the Bible, by means of its narrative, is a medium of exchange. We are being called

105

into a conversation, invited to bring our voices into that conversation, within the narrative interchange afforded by story. Both ours and the Bible's story are enriched by the process. Meanings will be created within the relationships established. Bridges of exchange will be forged across the years as we connect with storytellers of old. Our faith is that the same God who inspired them, inspires us as we share an interpretive community across the centuries. The truth we encounter at its most powerful is relational and experiential. It draws us into connection.

We also noted above that the movement of this book takes its clue from archaeology. Excavating a tell requires that the archaeologist begins at the top of a mound, which is the period of its latest date. As the search proceeds through the strata into the heart of the mound, one works backward through time. Once the excavator reaches bedrock, it becomes possible to reconstruct a history of the tell, reorganizing the data into a meaningful, interpretive whole. If we adopt the metaphor of the Hebrew Bible as a stratified mound of literary data, like the archaeologist, the literary critic can proceed through the literary strata backward in time, organizing the data around centers of meaning identified within the respective strata.

Our goal has been to take sacred story seriously as a means to communicate truth about one's knowledge of the spiritual life; to locate a center of meaning within the various strata, and then from the perspective of that stance, to fill out the implications for understanding the spiritual life. We have discussed the Aaronid Zadokite story in Chronicles, the Mushite Levite story in Samuel/Kings, and the story of the Yahwist, who, though not a priest, had a perspective on Levi and Levites. We saw too that the Elohist and Priestly writers further reflect Mushite Levite tradition in the north (E) and Aaronid Zadokite tradition in the south (P). Following Friedman, we proposed that the JEP sources were combined to form a second edition of the Bible during the reign of Hezekiah as Mushite Levite priests were among those who fled south seeking refuge from Assyria's invasion of Israel.

Apocalyptic offers us an opportunity to summarize the priestly contribution to Israel's spiritual vision. There is a sense that apocalyptic is a genre that people, including priests, reach for when they hit rock bottom. This is our bedrock. With the fall of Israel (721 B.C.E.) and then Judah (587 B.C.E.), the institutional support of the priestly houses was gone. Established patterns for explanation were no longer in place. The initial thrust of apocalyptic is to reach even further into the traditional past for grounding, to the creation narrative itself, to find a logic to make sense of a chaotic present. This is the bedrock we have been referring to in our metaphor of the Hebrew Bible as a stratified mound of literary data. The foundation of later institutional systems rests on creation stories that explained how things came to be.

For those who believed that Jerusalem would never fall and were locked into that single plane of perception, the only result could be despair. It is our agenda for this chapter to trace how writers within each priestly family were able to shift perspective by moving within the tools of their sacred stories to engage the threat of collapse that invasion posed. Story became a medium of exchange that enabled hidden options to emerge as new possibilities. We will be looking for evidence of voice from our priestly families among the writers of the exilic and early postexilic period. It is no accident that the books of Isaiah, Ezekiel, and Jeremiah are among the longest books in the Bible. They were wrestling with issues that touched the very foundation of ancient Israelite existence.

To anticipate some of our conclusions: (1) The genius of sixth-century Isaiah and the writings of early apocalyptic found in the Isaianic corpus was the blending of forms orginating in different groups. God was perceived as breaking through established boundaries, offering the faithful a new seeing. As Isaiah suggested, a new song was being sung (Isa. 42:10). (2) A Zadokite Aaronid reading of God's action in the events of Judah's collapse are reflected in the apocalyptic visions of Ezekiel. Note particularly his visions of a restored temple and resurrected united kingdom. Later, Persian intervention in the politics of Yehud resolved the hierarchical tension between priestly families by lending its support to Ezekiel's proposal of "priests [Aaronid Zadokites] and Levites [Mushite]." This latter formula, as we have seen, was central to the Chronicler's work. (3) Although the Levites were viewed by Zadokites in Chronicles as second-class priests, apocalyptic was the genre that carried the full priestly voice of those Levitical families who traced their lineage back to Moses. That the Jewish canon of scripture ends with the book of Chronicles and the Christian Old Testament ends with Malachi, points to a bridge to an emergent Judaism and early Christianity of the late Second Temple period. These open a door for us to discuss the Jewishness of Jesus.

The Isaianic School of Prophecy

Scholars have long noted that material in the present book of Isaiah contains material that extends over 200 years: Isaiah's call, in 6:1, is dated to the "year Uzziah died" (734 B.C.E.) and later, in Isaiah 45:1, there is reference to Cyrus of Persia (538 B.C.E.) as God's anointed. Some have proposed that we think of the material in Isaiah as the literary product of a school of disciples gathered in the name of the founder. Periodically, anonymous writers from the school would add material to the corpus to extend the teachings of the founder to subsequent time periods. This has led to such designations as 1 Isaiah of the eighth century, 2 Isaiah of the sixth century, and 3 Isaiah toward the beginning of the postexilic period. Isaiah 34—35 and 40—55 are often designated as writings dated to the sixth century; these deal with the fall of Judah. Isaiah 24—27 are writings that begin to move into the genre of apocalyptic. Isaiah 56—66 reflects a growing conflict among priestly leaders that fits our reconstruction of Mushite and Zadokite tensions.[1]

A study of the Isaianic materials makes it clear that while we normally think of prophecy and apocalyptic as genres oriented toward the future, they are modes of thinking that are, at least initially, oriented to the past. Once having identified a pattern rooted in a traditional past, it becomes normative for an interpretation of the present and immediate future guided by the logic of the pattern identified. Even in terms of poetic style, it could be demonstrated that 2 Isaiah and the writer of Isaiah 24—27 were reaching back into ancient literary forms in search of a regrounding at a time when all things present were under threat.[2]

As long as established institutions are in place, there is a context for interpretation. One can turn to identifiable leaders for explanations of God's actions. But when all that is swept away, as in the invasion and destruction of a city, where does one turn? We know that eighth-century Isaiah shared a central affirmation of the royal theology that Jerusalem would never fall. It was YHWH's city, and YHWH ruled the universe.

---

[1]For a treatment of Isaiah 56—66, see Paul D. Hanson, *The Dawn of Apocalyptic: The Historical and Sociological Roots of Jewish Apocalyptic Eschatology*, rev. ed. (Philadelphia: Fortress Press, 1979).

[2]See William R. Millar, *Isaiah 24—27 and the Origin of Apocalyptic*, Harvard Semitic Monograph Series 11 (Missoula, Mont.: Scholars Press, 1976). The biblical translation for texts from Isaiah 24—27 are drawn from this book.

Ancient Near Eastern creation stories conceived of the origin of the universe within a mythic pattern that could be described briefly as moving from threat–war–victory–feast. In a number of ancient Near Eastern cultures, the universe was conceived as containing within its boundaries the destructive powers of chaos. They lived with the constant threat of its resurgence to center stage. A flood could wipe out a village built too close to a river. An invading army could destroy a town. A deadly disease could quietly decimate a population.

It was the responsibility of a creator god to engage the threatening power of chaos and, as in war, subdue its destructive energy and contain it within created boundaries, making the world safe for habitation. The victory would be celebrated at a cosmic feast centered at the god's house at key points in the religious calendar—like the new year.

Israel too had its version of that ancient story of creation. So that when sixth-century Isaiah, so-called 2 Isaiah, faced the reality of Jerusalem's destruction, those grounded in the thinking of the Isaianic school faced a crisis that was not only political and military, but theological as well. If their plane of perception, reading God's actions in the events of their day, was locked into the belief that Jerusalem would never fall, the fact that it had fallen demanded explanation. If they were to come up with an insight that moved them beyond despair, they would have to shift their perspective on the events of the day.

At such times, it would not do to try something brand new, unfamiliar, and untried. The natural response would be to reach back into one's established tradition looking for clues that for the moment might be hidden from view. As evident in 2 Isaiah and in Isaiah 24–27, apocalyptic is a genre within which the old language—poetic style and content—of original time resurfaced.

If, as we have been suggesting in this study, that biblical narrative is and was a medium of exchange, it offers us an approach to a reading of the text and for understanding the early stages of apocalyptic. If we carry our hypothesis that Mushite Levites were a support group into our reading of the Isaianic materials, we can see how their story has helped shape some of the Isaianic vision. When we discussed the Deuteronomist's presentation of Hezekiah, who faced the threat of Assyria in Kings, for instance, we suggested that the narrator was drawing on resources from the royal belief that Zion was safe as well from the Mosaic vision of freedom in the wilderness.

If there were Mushite Levites in conversation with those of the Isaianic school, that interchange could have produced much of what we see in the Isaianic materials. The centrality of Zion was part of the discourse, but so also was the theme of a second exodus delivering the faithful from threat. In Isaiah 24—27, we can see how the creation pattern of threat–war–victory–feast was a discernible organizing principle being affirmed about God's activity in their present. There was a reaching back for grounding. That grounding was found in ancient creation language, and the logic of the creation pattern guided their reading of the present. What was hidden from those locked into the belief that Zion would never fall was the long-held insight from groups like the Mushite Levites that there are resources for healing even in the wilderness experiences of life. The God who led Israel through the first wilderness could lead them through a second wilderness.

The genius of sixth-century Isaiah and the writings of early apocalyptic was the blending of forms originating in different groups. God was breaking through established boundaries offering the faithful a new seeing. As Isaiah suggested, a new song was being sung (Isa. 42:10).

Isaiah 24:16b—25:9

Let us assume that Jerusalem had recently fallen to the Babylonians. God's holy city was gone. Many of the faithful not already in hiding or killed were somewhere in the process of being exiled to Babylon. The challenge facing the Isaiah of the sixth century was to draw on the resources of his prophetic school to discern the hand of God in the events they were facing. Our thesis is that in the group were Mushite Levites with a long history of life in the desolate places. They, raised on the belief of the invincibility of Zion, in conversation with others in the school needed to hammer out together a vision that moved beyond understanding the event as simply punishment from God. Already in the Suffering Servant passages we have 2 Isaiah developing the idea that in the very suffering of the servant Israel, they were becoming a light to the nations. Our purpose in taking a closer look at this text from the Isaianic apocalypse (24—27) is to illustrate how the Mushite Levite voice could live on precisely because they knew the ways of the wilderness. The passage selected to examine has been shaped by the mythic pattern of the ancient creation myth discussed above.

Threat (Isaiah 24:16b–18b)

Some say, "I am wasted!"
"I am wasted! Oh, woe is me!"

"The treacherous are treacherous.
With treachery, they are treacherous."

Pack and Snare and Pit
Against you, inhabitants of the land.

He who flees from the marauding Pack,
He falls in the Pit.

He who climbs out of the Pit,
He is caught in the Snare. (Isaiah 24:17)

Even in poetic contexts, we see that the literary device of speech within speech can be employed. Psychologically, this is extremely important because it means voice still has the capacity for movement within the narrative world. Above all, the function of narrative is to structure meaning that makes sense out of events experienced. Once it becomes frozen in one plane of perception whose explanation is not convincing, it becomes dysfunctional.

The narrator acknowledges the pain of those suffering at the hands of the invaders. The alliteration and repetition in the Hebrew, even through the sound of the words themselves, drives the point home. Then the narrator observes that there appears to be no escape. Pack and snare and pit are all against us. We flee the marauding pack, and we fall into a pit. We climb out of a pit and are caught in a snare. The land is on the verge of panic, one of the characteristics of chaos itself.

War (Isaiah 24:18c–23)

The windows of heaven are opened.
The foundations of earth do tremble.

Earth is broken in pieces.
Earth is rent asunder.
Earth is violently shaken.

Earth quivers like a drunk.
It sways like a hut.

But it shall be in that day:
Yahweh will charge the gods in heaven;
The kings of the earth on earth.

They will be gathered as a group to the Pit.
They will be locked up as a prisoner in the Dungeon.
In due time, they will be punished.

The Moon will be confounded; the Sun abashed.
Yahweh of Hosts will reign at Mount Zion.
And opposite His elders, in Jerusalem, the Kabod.

The biggest challenge facing an interpreter of a devastation as extensive as the fall of one's homeland is to find positive meaning in the violence. The ancient creation story being drawn upon envisions a divine warrior taking on the power of chaos itself. Since it is a cosmic confrontation, the very foundations of earth itself will tremble. Of course, we who are mere mortals cannot help but be overwhelmed by it all. So in apocalyptic settings, the narrator has shifted the perspective from an account of a contained historical battle to one of cosmic proportions. In the shift to the geography of the universe itself, hidden possibilities for explanation begin to emerge.

The windows of heaven are opened. The solid firmament has windows protecting us from the blue waters of chaos overhead; but as in the days of Noah and the flood, those windows are opened and the water above pours in. The foundations of the earth tremble. As the protective bubble that surrounds the earth gives way, the earth is broken in pieces, rent asunder, violently shaken. The earth quivers like a drunk, sways like a hut.

To be sure, war does that to an organized society. But if we understand world to also mean what today we might call a social world of meaning, when that gives way and we no longer have the categories to make sense out of things, the foundations of our sense of who and why we are also break into pieces and are rent asunder.

The ground for hope, deriving from the creation story affirming a divine warrior making the universe safe for a created order, is Yahweh charging from his place to take on the gods of heaven and the kings of earth. Those who would unleash chaos are gathered into a pit and locked in a dungeon. In due time they will be punished. The sun and moon as witnesses to the cosmic scope of events stand abashed; even they are amazed. So while it may look like Zion has been abandoned by Yahweh, he will reclaim his throne: "Yahweh of Hosts will reign at Mount Zion. And opposite his elders, in Jerusalem, the Kabod," that is, the manifestation of his presence.

Victory (Isaiah 25:1–4)

Yahweh, You are my God!
I lift You up; I praise Your name!

You have given counsels of wonder;
From of old, perfect faithfulness.

Therefore, people of strength will worship You;
Haughty nations revere You.

For You are a refuge to the poor,
A refuge to the needy.
A shelter from the winter; shade from the heat.

"From of old, perfect faithfulness." Once the paradigm has been reidentified, its logic becomes the guide for reading current events. Though we may stand yet in the midst of war, we know on a pattern from of old, that Yahweh will reestablish his throne at Zion. Once more he will be a refuge to the poor and to the needy. He will be a shelter from the winter and shade from the heat. Those who currently appear strong and haughty will one day acknowledge the power and place of the real ruler of the universe.

Feast (Isaiah 25:6–8)

Yahweh of Hosts has made
For all peoples on this mount:

A feast of oil;
A feast of wine;

Fat, well cured;
The best of wine.

He will swallow on this mount
The net ensnared
About all the people;

The web woven
About all the nations.
He will swallow Death forever.

He will wipe the tears
From all faces.

The reproach of his people he will remove
From all the earth.

Death, or *Mot* in Hebrew, who is also one of the gods of chaos known from Canaanite tradition, will be swallowed up. In the Canaanite context it is Mot who swallows up the forces of life as evidenced by the onset of winter in the cycle of the seasons. Here, however, the affirmation is that Yahweh in the cosmic battle being engaged will swallow up death at the great feast to celebrate victory on the mountain. All the tears of the faithful will be wiped away. The reproach of Yahweh's people will be removed from all the earth.

Evidence that the Isaianic vision draws much of its inspiration from values focused on the world of relationships—as we have suggested was central to the Mushite Levite tradition—is Isaiah 60 with its description of a restored Jerusalem: "I will appoint Peace as your overseer and Righteousness as your taskmaster. Violence shall no more be heard in your land, devastation or destruction within your borders; you shall call your walls Salvation, and your gates Praise" (Isa. 60:17b–18); then the famous passage, thoroughly at home in the Mushite tradition: "He has sent me to bring good news to the oppressed, to bind up the brokenhearted, to proclaim liberty to the captives and release to the prisoners...you shall be called priests of the LORD, you shall be named ministers of our God" (Isa. 61:1, 6a).

Ezekiel

It is from Ezekiel that we hear again the Aaronid Zadokite voice. Ezekiel too was a priest who lived through the final days of Judah and was probably among those exiled to Babylon during the first deportation (597 B.C.E.). "[Nebuchadnezzar]...deported Jehoiachin to Babylon; and the king's mother and wives and officers and the notables were brought as exiles from Jerusalem to Babylon" (2 Kgs. 24:15). "In the thirtieth year, in the fourth month, on the fifth day of the month, I was among the exiles by the river Chebar...the word of the LORD came to the priest Ezekiel" (Ezek. 1:1–2).

Recent scholars studying apocalyptic have argued that it need not be a genre only for the poor and outcast. It can also be a genre for the educated elite. Apocalyptic visions are frequently highly complex and sophisticated creations that give evidence of authors deeply familiar with the inner dynamics of multiple traditions operative in their cultures.[3] Since Ezekiel was a Zadokite priest, we should not be surprised that his writings include some apocalyptic passages. The loss of access to the temple would be an experience of extreme crisis for such a person, since God's house in Jerusalem was the center of the Zadokite faith vision.

In Chronicles we noted that the author did not appear to interpret the fall of Judah as a fall. Such a concept would conflict with the fundamental belief that Jerusalem was God's holy city and would never fall. But the Chronicler, consistent with a politics of purity, did acknowledge that the city had been corrupted by the actions of some kings and the people. It was in need of purification. That was being accomplished by the sabbath principle. The land needed time to receive its Sabbaths. Thus, the seventy years between the first and second temples was a time when the land was renewing itself.

If we move earlier to the time of Ezekiel, we see visions of a restoration and resurrection that speak of replacing what now appears to be gone. This mode of spirituality argues that in times of crisis, we are called upon to "believe anyway." The truths taught during the many years of the First Temple still hold.

Valley of Dry Bones (Ezek. 37)

In one vision, Ezekiel was taken by the spirit to a valley full of bones that were very dry. It would not be unexpected that some of the faithful on a forced march from Jerusalem to Babylon could well have marched through a valley of bones. There were battles in the last days of Judah and, before there was time to clean up and bury the dead, animals and birds of prey could have reduced the bodies of slain soldiers to a valley of bones. For Ezekiel, such a sight captured at a glance what was on everyone's minds: "Mortal, these bones are the whole house of Israel. They say, 'Our bones are dried up, and our hope is lost; we are cut off completely'" (Ezek. 37:11).

In Babylon, either in camps or at forced labor, a priest like Ezekiel no doubt felt called to say the encouraging word to those about him

---

[3]See Jon L. Berquist, *Judaism in Persia's Shadow: A Social and Historical Approach* (Minneapolis: Fortress Press, 1995), 177–92; and Paula McNutt, *Reconstructing the Society of Ancient Israel,* Library of Ancient Israel (Louisville, Ky.: Westminster John Knox Press, 1999), 212.

lost in despair. Sometimes when we are discouraged, even if food is available, we may see no point in eating and become quite literally a bag of bones.

"[God] said, 'Mortal, can these bones live?' I answered, 'O Lord God, you know.' Then he said to me, 'Prophesy to these bones, and say to them: O dry bones, hear the word of the LORD. Thus says the Lord GOD to these bones: I will cause breath to enter you, and you shall live. I will lay sinews on you, and will cause flesh to come upon you, and cover you with skin, and put breath in you, and you shall live; and you shall know that I am the LORD'" (Ezek. 37:3–6).

We have all seen World War II pictures of scenes in concentration camps filled with emaciated bodies. If we can imagine Ezekiel addressing such despairing folk, he is reaching for that part of them that would dare to hope their nation could live again. "Thus says the Lord GOD: I am going to open your graves, and bring you up from your graves, O my people; and I will bring you back to the land of Israel. And you shall know that I am the LORD, when I open your graves, and bring you up from your graves, O my people. I will put my spirit within you, and you shall live, and I will place you on your own soil; then you shall know that I, the LORD, have spoken and will act" (Ezek. 37:12–14).

This is resurrection language. As interpreted by the text itself, what will resurrect is not the literal dry bones that have triggered the vision; rather it is the nation that the image represents that will resurrect. The very despair of the people in exile is the grave. Ezekiel, by means of the spoken word, is engaging that despair and appealing to a deeper hope that reemerges as he shifts the perspective on the series of events.

It becomes clear as Ezekiel continues that his vision of the restored Israel is to return to the days of the united monarchy under David and Solomon. He sees two sticks: one named Judah and one named Ephraim. "Join them together into one stick, so that they may become one in your hand…Never again shall they be two nations, and never again shall they be divided into two kingdoms" (Ezek. 37:15–22).

Allusions to the ancient creation story resurface in Ezekiel's account of Gog's attack on a tranquil people in a peaceful land. Yahweh's anger is kindled as he rises to fight Gog. "On that day there shall be a great shaking in the land of Israel; the fish of the sea, and the birds of the the air, and the animals of the field, and all creeping things that creep on the ground, and all human beings that are on the face of the earth, shall quake at my presence, and the mountains shall be thrown down, and the cliffs shall fall, and every wall shall tumble to the ground" (Ezek. 38:19–20). Yahweh will be victor and there shall be a great feast as all the winged birds and wild beasts are called to consume what is left of the army of Gog. "I will display my glory among the nations" (Ezek. 39:17–21). "Now I will restore the fortunes of Jacob" (Ezek. 39:25).

Ezekiel 40—48

In our discussion of Josiah within the context of the Kings narrative, we suggested that given the names of those mentioned in positions of leadership in Kings and in the book of Jeremiah, who himself was a Mushite Levite priest, it could be that Josiah was more open than earlier kings had been to allowing Mushite Levite priests to serve at the temple of Jerusalem. The book found in the temple, which precipitated the reforms of Josiah, was a northern document connected with what we now know as Deuteronomy. We also suggested that the fall of Nineveh in 612 would have confirmed for many that Yahweh was pleased with the actions of Josiah.

The killing of Josiah by Pharaoh Neco in 609 B.C.E. came as a shock to many. It is conceivable that Zadokite priests, however, read the event as confirmation from Yahweh of their concern that only Aaronid Zadokites are to be full-fledged priests allowed to mount the altar. In Ezekiel's vision of a restored Jerusalem, he is quite clear about who will be in charge of the resurrected temple. "The levitical priests, the descendants of Zadok, who kept the charge of my sanctuary when the people of Israel went astray from me, shall come near to me to minister to me; and they shall attend me to offer me the fat and the blood, says the Lord GOD. It is they who shall enter my sanctuary, it is they who shall approach my table, to minister me, and they shall keep my charge" (Ezek. 44:15–16).

Ezekiel proposed that the purity codes of old be enforced with renewed vigor, since the anger of Yahweh was high. "No foreigner, uncircumcised in heart and flesh, of all the foreigners who are among the people of Israel, shall enter my sanctuary" (Ezek. 44:9). Even the [Mushite] Levites were to be kept away from the most sacred places. "They shall not come near to me, to serve me as priest, nor come near any of my sacred offerings, the things that are most sacred; but they shall bear their shame, and the consequences of the abominations that they have committed. Yet I will appoint them to keep charge of the temple, to do all its chores, all that is to be done in it" (Ezek. 44:13–14). Much of Ezekiel 44 lists in great detail purity stipulations that were binding on Zadokite priests to maintain the purity of God's house. With the temple restored, healing waters will go forth into the land, going to such places as the Dead Sea to restore life there. Not only will there be fish in the sea, but the banks will be surrounded by trees. "Their fruit will be for food, and their leaves for healing" (Ezek. 47:12).

As we saw in our discussion of Chronicles, this division of priest and Levite was assumed as a matter of course. It was also suggested that the Persians lent their support to the Aaronid Zadokites by granting them permission to run the internal affairs of the Second Temple. This gave the Zadokites the political power they needed to enforce what Ezekiel may only have envisioned as a solution.

Malachi

The last book in the Christian canon of the Old Testament is Malachi. The last book in the Jewish canon of the Hebrew Bible is Chronicles. Because Chronicles is placed last, the closing statement in the Hebrew Bible is one of hope for Jews about to embark on the challenges of the Second Temple period. Cyrus the Persian has just announced, "All the kingdoms of the earth YHWH the God of heaven has given to me, and he has charged me to build for him a house in Jerusalem which is in Judah. Who among you [is] from any of his people? May YHWH his God [be] with him, and let him go up" (2 Chron. 36:23). With the Zadokites in charge of the Second Temple, such a text opens the pathway for an endorsement of their position as priests. For the Chronicler, the tension between the priestly houses of Mushite Levites and Aaronid Zadokites has been settled. The priests are Zadokites and the Levites are to be of service to the sons of Aaron.

Malachi, however, offers us a different picture of the situation. In spite of the many years that have transpired since the days when Solomon dismissed Abiathar, Levites still claimed their right to be called to full-fledged priesthood. In a book that is usually dated to the early Second Temple period,[4] we have in Malachi the practice of priests

---

[4]See Paul D. Hanson, *The People Called: The Growth of Community in the Bible* (San Francisco: Harper & Row, 1986), 277–87; and Julia M. O'Brien, *Priest and Levite in Malachi* (Atlanta: Society of Biblical Literature, 1990).

in power being criticized. "And now, O priests, this command is for you. If you will not listen, if you will not lay it to heart to give glory to my name, says the LORD of hosts, then I will send the curse on you and I will curse your blessings; indeed I have already cursed them, because you do not lay it to heart. I will rebuke your offspring, and spread dung on your faces, the dung of your offerings, and I will put you out of my presence" (Mal. 2:1–3).

There follows an affirmation that God's covenant with Levi will endure. The issue seems to be that those currently filling the levitical office of priest—and all priests are of the tribe of Levi—are not meeting God's standards. God is about to purge the corruption from their midst: "He will purify the descendants of Levi and refine them like gold and silver, until they present offerings to the Lord in righteousness" (Mal. 3:3).

There is the memory of a time when the covenant was held up, probably a time when Mushite Levites were allowed to hold priestly office. "My covenant with him [Levi] was a covenant of life and well-being, which I gave him; this called for reverence, and he revered me and stood in awe of my name. True instruction was in his mouth, and no wrong was found on his lips. He walked with me in integrity and uprightness, and he turned many from iniquity. For the lips of a priest should guard knowledge, and people should seek instruction from his mouth, for he is the messenger [*malach*] of the LORD of hosts" (Mal. 2:5–7).

Among the complaints against the priests in power were traditional concerns of those in Mushite tradition. "[You] subvert [the cause of] the widow, orphan, and stranger, said the LORD of Hosts," (Mal. 3:5, JPS). "Remember the teaching of my servant Moses, the statutes and ordinances that I commanded him at Horeb for all Israel" (Mal. 4:4). The mention of both Moses and Horeb is language of Deuteronomic tradition. Then there is the reference to Elijah, who we have already discussed as a new Moses appearing in the dark days of Ahab. "I will send you the prophet Elijah before the great and terrible day of the LORD comes" (Mal. 4:5).

It becomes clear why the Christian canon of the Old Testament should reorder the books of the Hebrew Bible to conclude with Malachi. Groundwork was being laid for a bridge to the New Testament narrative. The gospel of Mark will quote Isaiah 40:1, modified by Malachi 3:1: "See, I am sending my messenger [*malachi*] to prepare the way before me" (Mal. 3:1). In Malachi's context this is in reference to YHWH's surprise visit to the temple to purge the descendants of Levi. In Mark, the reference is to John the Baptist—a messenger in the wilderness—preparing the way for Jesus' coming. In addition, we note that Elijah is a key figure appearing many times in the New Testament story. When one considers the ministry of Jesus, we see many of the same values and concerns that have been carried by the Mushite Levites finding renewed expression in the life of Jesus. When we consider that the Hebrew word *Zadokite* translates into Sadducee in the Greek, we see the ancient tension between two kinds of spirituality once again central, this time within New Testament narrative.[5]

The Jewishness of Jesus

In the introduction to this book, we raised the question, Why should we care about the priestly narratives of the Hebrew Bible, those sacred texts Christians call the Old Testament? Hasn't all that been replaced by the spirituality of Jesus and the New Testament? At the time we didn't directly address the question, but we are now ready to speak to the issue.

We live in a very fortunate time for New Testament study. Two remarkable libraries discovered by archaeologists in the 1940s are now becoming readily available to general audiences in English translation. One library of Christian gnostic texts, including some previously unknown Christian gospels, was discovered in Egypt at a place called Nag Hammadi that has opened up a window to the diversity of Christian expression available in the early Christian centuries. They offer us new insight into the process of how doctrine was formulated, leading up to the councils authorized by Constantine.

In addition, the library of a group who called themselves sons of Zadok gathered at the Dead Sea has been discovered, dated to the days of the Maccabean revolt and the Roman occupation of Palestine. This was a community in existence during Jesus' lifetime and, among other things, the library reveals to us the nature of the biblical text available at the time. Needless to say, biblical studies in both Old and New Testament have received a significant boost with these new materials at hand. We are discovering afresh how rich the cultural

---

[5]Marcus J. Borg has made very effective use of the categories of politics of purity and politics of compassion in his analysis of the Jesus of history in his work *Conflict, Holiness, and Politics in the Teachings of Jesus* (Harrisburg, Pa.: Trinity Press International, 1984, 1998).

diversity of Judaism was during Jesus' day and how much of his teaching and ministry can be interpreted within the political and religious challenges of the time.

A third resource for approaching the Jewishness of Jesus, often overlooked perhaps because it is right under our noses, is the Old Testament itself. Not only were Jesus' interpreters deeply immersed in these stories producing what scholars have called the history of the Christ of faith, or the post-Easter Jesus; we can safely assume that Jesus knew these stories too. What we call the Old Testament was Jesus' Bible. In the spirit of getting to know someone through the books he read, we have before us a resource for what has been called the historical Jesus, or the pre-Easter Jesus, to use the language of Marcus Borg.

Our reading of the priestly traditions of the Hebrew Bible is yet another point of entry to an understanding of the Jesus of history. The social situation we described for the Chronicler was one which called for the study of the First Temple period with renewed energy at a time when Palestine was a colony of the Persian Empire. Priestly leaders were looking for clues about God's activity in the world. This was the same kind of social situation Jesus faced. Palestine was a Roman colony engaged with many of the same political problems the Chronicler encountered. The same Second Temple the Chronicler wrote about was still standing in Jerusalem, made even more elaborate by Herod. Jesus too would have understood the importance of carving out a sacred place within which to tell one's own story in one's own words.

But Jesus also knew what it was like to live on the margins of the social order. He didn't have to dream up a concern for vulnerable ones like widows, orphans, and strangers. The descendants of Abiathar had already filled his Bible with such stories. One learned much about the wilderness experience from those we have been calling Mushite Levites. Who did Jesus' followers connect Jesus with on the Mount of Transfiguration but Moses and Elijah? Jesus too is one who humanized the narrative, named the powers, and understood the holy in terms of healing. His parables are masterful creations in the art of drawing people into a medium of exchange, of beginning with the very familiar, but then encouraging people to see the world in a new way.

That the Hebrew Bible contains the stories and teachings of two priestly families with their respective spiritual pathways should caution us against picking one over the other. Each has its place in its own social situation. That they are in tension calls us to be ever vigilant on our own journey; indeed, that tension gives us a creative context within which to make sense of our own pathway. We, just as Jesus did in his day, draw on the wisdom of both so that in our speaking and acting, the spirit may become manifest in our own life and time.

Scripture Index